JAMES

J. Vernon McGee

THOMAS NELSON PUBLISHERS

Nashville

Published in Nashville, Tennessee, by Thomas Nelson, Inc., and distributed in Canada by Lawson Falle, Ltd., Cambridge, Ontario.

Quotation from *The Salt Cellars* (2 vols.) by Charles Haddon Spurgeon. Pilgrim Publications, Pasadena, Texas. Used by permission.

Scripture quotations are from the KING JAMES VERSION of the Bible.

Library of Congress Cataloging-in-Publication Data

McGee, J. Vernon (John Vernon), 1904–1988
    [Thru the Bible with J. Vernon McGee]
    Thru the Bible commentary series / J. Vernon McGee.
        p.   cm.
    Reprint. Originally published: Thru the Bible with J. Vernon McGee. 1975.
    Includes bibliographical references.
    ISBN 0-8407-3306-2
    1. Bible—Commentaries.   I. Title.
BS491.2.M37   1991
220.7'7—dc20

90–41340
CIP

Printed in the United States of America

1 2 3 4 5 6 7 — 96 95 94 93 92 91

CONTENTS

JAMES

PREFACE

The radio broadcasts of the Thru the Bible Radio five-year program were transcribed, edited, and published first in single-volume paperbacks to accommodate the radio audience.

There has been a minimal amount of further editing for this publication. Therefore, these messages are not the word-for-word recording of the taped messages which went out over the air. The changes were necessary to accommodate a reading audience rather than a listening audience.

These are popular messages, prepared originally for a radio audience. They should not be considered a commentary on the entire Bible in any sense of that term. These messages are devoid of any attempt to present a theological or technical commentary on the Bible. Behind these messages is a great deal of research and study in order to interpret the Bible from a popular rather than from a scholarly (and too-often boring) viewpoint.

We have definitely and deliberately attempted "to put the cookies on the bottom shelf so that the kiddies could get them."

The fact that these messages have been translated into many languages for radio broadcasting and have been received with enthusiasm reveals the need for a simple teaching of the whole Bible for the masses of the world.

I am indebted to many people and to many sources for bringing this volume into existence. I should express my especial thanks to my secretary, Gertrude Cutler, who supervised the editorial work; to Dr. Elliott R. Cole, my associate, who handled all the detailed work with the publishers; and finally, to my wife Ruth for tenaciously encouraging me from the beginning to put my notes and messages into printed form.

Solomon wrote, ". . . of making many books there is no end; and much study is a weariness of the flesh" (Eccl. 12:12). On a sea of books that flood the marketplace, we launch this series of THRU THE BIBLE with the hope that it might draw many to the one Book, *The Bible*.

J. Vernon McGee

JAMES

The General Epistle of

JAMES

INTRODUCTION

The Epistle of James is the first in a group of epistles customarily called General Epistles, which includes James, 1 and 2 Peter, 1, 2, and 3 John, and Jude. They are designated as general or "catholic" epistles in the sense that they are universal, not being addressed to any particular individual or church, but to the church as a whole.

The problem of authorship is a major one. There is no question that James wrote the Epistle of James, but *which* James was the author? Some find at least four men by the name of James in the New Testament. I believe that you can find three who are clearly identified:

1. James, the brother of John and one of the sons of Zebedee. These two men were called "sons of thunder" by our Lord (see Mark 3:17). He was slain by Herod who at the same time put Simon Peter into prison (see Acts 12:1–2).

2. James, the son of Alphaeus, called "James the less" (see Mark 15:40). He is mentioned in the list of apostles, but very little is known concerning him. I automatically dismiss him as the author of this epistle.

3. James, the Lord's brother. He was a son of Mary and of Joseph, which made him a half brother of the Lord Jesus. In Matthew 13:55 we read: "Is not this the carpenter's son? is not his mother called Mary? and his brethren, James, and Joses, and Simon, and Judas?" In the beginning, the Lord's brethren did not believe in Him at all, but the time came when James became head of the church at Jerusalem. In Acts 15 James seems to have presided over that great council in Jerusa-

lem. At least he made the summation and brought the council to a decision under the leading of the Holy Spirit. I believe it was this James whom Paul referred to in Galatians 2:9, "And when James, Cephas, and John, who seemed to be pillars, perceived the grace that was given unto me, they gave to me and Barnabas the right hands of fellowship; that we should go unto the heathen, and they unto the circumcision." This James is the man whom we believe to be the author of this epistle.

This epistle was written about A.D. 45–50. There have been those who have said that James wrote his epistle to combat the teachings of Paul; they argue that James emphasizes works while Paul emphasizes faith. However, the earliest of Paul's epistles, 1 Thessalonians, was written about A.D. 52–56. Therefore, even Paul's first epistle was not written until after the Epistle of James, which was the first book of the New Testament to be written.

It is clear that James' theme is not works, but faith—the same as Paul's theme, but James emphasizes what faith produces. Both James and Paul speak a great deal of faith *and* works. They give us the two aspects of justification by faith, both of which are clear in the writings of Paul:

1. *Faith*—we are not justified *by* works. Paul wrote, "For by grace are ye saved through faith; and that not of yourselves: it is the gift of God: Not of works, lest any man should boast" (Eph. 2:8–9). And he also wrote, "Not by works of righteousness which we have done, but according to his mercy he saved us . . ." (Titus 3:5).

2. *Works*—we are justified *for* works. In Titus 3:8 Paul says, "This is a faithful saying, and these things I will that thou affirm constantly, that they which have believed in God might be careful to maintain good works. . . ." In Ephesians 2:10 he tells us, "For we are his workmanship, created in Christ Jesus unto good works, which God hath before ordained that we should walk in them."

Faith is the *root* of salvation—Paul emphasizes that; works are the *fruit* of salvation—that is the thing James emphasizes. Or, we can express it this way: Faith is the cause of salvation, and works are the *result* of salvation.

When Paul says that works will not save you, he is talking about the works of the Law. When James emphasizes that works are essential, he is talking about works of faith, not works of the Law. He said, "Yea, a man may say, Thou hast faith, and I have works: shew me thy faith without thy works, and I will shew thee my faith by my works" (James 2:18). God looks down and sees your heart, and He knows whether you believe or not—that is justification by faith. But your neighbor next door doesn't see your heart; he can only judge by your works, the *fruit* of your faith.

The following are what I consider to be the two key verses of this epistle. "But be ye doers of the word, and not hearers only, deceiving your own selves" (James 1:22). "But wilt thou know, O vain man, that faith without works is dead?" (James 2:20).

The Epistle of James deals with the ethics of Christianity, not doctrine. He is really going to bear down on the practical, but he will not get away from the subject of faith. James was evidently a very practical individual. Tradition says that he was given the name "Old Camel Knees" because he spent so much time in prayer.

Due to its practical nature, this epistle has been compared to the Book of Proverbs as well as to the Sermon on the Mount. James argues that justification by faith is demonstrated by works; it must be poured into the test tube of works (ch. 1—2), of words (ch.3), of worldliness (ch. 4), and of a warning to the rich (ch. 5).

OUTLINE

I. **Verification of Genuine Faith, Chapters 1—3**
  A. God Tests Faith by Trials, Chapter 1:1–12
     (Twofold result: development of patience here, v. 3; reward hereafter, v. 12.)
  B. God Does Not Test Faith with Evil, Chapter 1:13–21
     (Evil comes from within—the flesh, v. 14.)
  C. God Tests Faith by THE WORD, Not by Man's Words, Chapter 1:22–27
     (Doing, not doctrine, is the final test of faith; knowing is not enough.)
  D. God Tests Faith by Attitude and Action in Respect of Persons, Chapter 2:1–13
  E. God Tests Faith by Good Works, Chapter 2:14–26
     (Abraham is an illustration of works, v. 21.)
  F. God Tests Faith by the Tongue, Chapter 3
     ("What is in the well of the heart will come up through the bucket of the mouth.")

II. **Vacuity and Vapidness of Worldliness, Chapter 4**
   (Worldliness is identified with fighting and the spirit of dissension, vv. 1–2.)

III. **Vexation of the Rich; Value of the Imminent Coming of Christ, Chapter 5**
    (The soon coming of Christ produces patience, vv. 7–8, and prayer, vv. 13–18.)
   A. Riches Are a Care (Rich Warned), Chapter 5:1–6
   B. The Comming of Christ Is a Comfort, Chapter 5:7–12
   C. The Prayer of the Righteous Is a Power, Chapter 5:13–20

CHAPTER 1

THEME: God tests faith by trials; God does not test
with evil; God tests faith by the Word, not by man's
words*

The Epistle of James is a very practical book which deals with the
ethics of Christianity rather than with doctrine. James will really
bear down on some practical issues, but the theme of faith is also seen
throughout his entire epistle. The emphasis in James is on the works
which are produced by faith. In the first three chapters he is going to
speak of the verification of genuine faith and give us some of the ways
God tests faith.

GOD TESTS FAITH BY TRIALS

**James, a servant of God and of the Lord Jesus Christ, to
the twelve tribes which are scattered abroad, greeting
[James 1:1].**

"James, a servant of God and of the Lord Jesus Christ." "Servant" is
literally a bond slave. Now I do not know about you, but I am confident
that if I had been the Lord's half brother on the human side, somewhere in this epistle I would have let you know that. I would have
brought in that fact in a very pious and humble way, but I surely would
have let you know. However, James does not do that. Instead, he calls
himself a bond slave of God and of the Lord Jesus Christ.

At first the Lord Jesus' human brethren did not believe He was the
Son of God. They had been brought up with Him and had played with
Him. They had seen Him grow. They noticed that He was unusual, but
they did not believe that He was the Savior of the world. Our Lord Jesus
was so human when He was here on this earth that even His own
brethren did not believe at the first. Of course, your family members
are always the hardest people to reach, yet they are the ones we should

reach. James came to know the Lord Jesus not only as his blood brother but as his own Savior, and then he became His bond slave. Notice what James calls Him—he uses His full name, the Lord Jesus Christ. James says, "He is my Lord." Jesus was His human name, and James knew Him as Jesus, his half brother; but he also knew Him as Christ, the Messiah who had come and had died for the sins of the world. Jesus was not just a name, but He was called Jesus because He would save His people from their sins.

"To the twelve tribes which are scattered abroad, greeting." It is obvious that James is referring to the believers in Israel. He is writing to the Christian Jews of that day. After all, the early church was 100 percent Jewish for quite a period of time. A few Gentiles became believers, and then a great revival broke out in the heart of the Roman Empire in the area of what is Turkey today. That is where the seven churches of Asia Minor were located. But James, evidently writing before this took place, is addressing the Jewish believers.

"To the twelve tribes which are scattered abroad." Today people speak of the "ten lost tribes of Israel," but no tribes really got lost. God scattered them throughout the world. They did not settle in England or the United States, although there are many Jews in both places. They are on every continent of the world. There is a tremendous Jewish population in Russia. There are some in China, some in Japan—they are "scattered abroad." James wrote this epistle to believing Jews of that day who were scattered abroad.

"Greeting"—that translation is a little stilted, for the word in the Greek literally means "rejoice." He writes to them and says, "Rejoice." James was not sour-tempered. James was a man with a lot of life in him.

Now James is going to speak of rejoicing under unusual circumstances—

My brethren, count it all joy when ye fall into divers temptations [James 1:2].

"Divers temptations" means various trials. In other words, when you are having trouble, don't start crying as if something terrible has happened to you. You are to *rejoice* and count it all joy that God is testing you in this way!

The question is often asked whether the Christian is to experience joy in depth in all the trials and tensions of life. Very frankly, the answer is no—that is not what James is saying here. It leads to unreality to say that you are reconciled to the will of God when troubles come to you when you really are not reconciled. People piously say they have accepted God's will yet go around with a long face and weep half the time. My friend, you are not reconciled to the will of God until you can rejoice.

James goes on to make it clear that God does not give us trouble for trouble's sake; it is not an end in itself.

> **Knowing this, that the trying of your faith worketh patience [James 1:3].**

God has a goal in mind—you can count on that. James is speaking here about the attitude of your heart toward your trouble. The Greek aorist tense used here suggests that the joy is the result of the trial. In Hebrews 12 we see that one method God uses in the life of the believer is chastening, which literally means "child training." Trials are meaningless, suffering is senseless, and testing is irrational unless there is some good purpose for them. God says there is a reason for them, and it is a good reason. "And we know that all things work together for good to them that love God, to them who are the called according to his purpose" (Rom. 8:28). When the external pressures of testing are upon us and we are placed in the fires of adversity and tragedy and suffering, the attitude of faith should be that God has permitted it for a purpose and He has a high and lofty goal in view. We can know that God is working something out in our lives.

I must hasten to add that this does not necessarily mean that we will *understand* what purpose God has in it. This is the test of *faith*. We walk by faith and not by sight. Someone in the Middle Ages said, "God nothing does, nor suffers to be done, but what we would ourselves, if we could see through all events of things as well as He."

What are some of the purposes served in the testing of faith? In this epistle, James says that testing is the proof positive of genuine faith. Let me use a rather homely illustration. Some years ago I had the privilege of leading to the Lord a secretary to one of the officers in a large airplane plant here in Southern California. On a number of occasions she asked me to speak to a Bible study class in that plant. While I was there I learned something of how airplanes are built. They start out by designing a new plane on the drawing board. Then blueprints are drawn up and models are made. The models are tested, and then construction begins. After about two years the first plane will roll off the assembly line. The question remains: Will it fly? Will it perform? Will it stand the test? So a test pilot must then put the plane through the paces up in the air. When the plane has proven to be all that the maker has said it is, there is confidence in the plane and the airlines will buy it. It is then brought to the airport where passengers will board it, and the plane thus becomes serviceable and useful. In the same sense, ore is brought to an assayer to prove that it is gold or that it is silver. He will put a fire under it and pour acid on it, and then he declares whether or not it is genuine. Likewise God puts faith to the test to prove that it is genuine. Someone has expressed it like this: "The acid of grief tests the coin of belief." There is a lot of truth in that.

God tests our faith for a purpose: "Knowing this, that the trying of your faith worketh patience." He tests us in order that He might produce patience in our lives.

> **But let patience have her perfect work, that ye may be perfect and entire, wanting nothing [James 1:4].**

It is patience which will make you a full-grown Christian, but how does God produce patience in you? The very interesting thing is that patience is the fruit of the Holy Spirit. You will never become patient by trying to be patient, but neither will the Holy Spirit place it on a silver platter and offer it to you as a gift. Patience comes through suffering and testing.

"But let patience have her perfect work, that ye may be perfect and entire, wanting nothing." You will never be a "perfect"—that is, a complete, fully mature—Christian without patience. Some Christians therefore have never really grown up but have remained babes. I made the statement as a pastor one Sunday morning that there were more babes in the church service than there were in the nursery downstairs. I tell you, I didn't get too many laughs from that comment. The difference, however, is that the babies in the nursery were beautiful, but the ones sitting in the church service were not very pretty. There is much clamoring and criticizing, turmoil and tension in our churches today. The reason is that many Christians have not grown up; they are still babes.

David wrote in Psalm 131, "LORD, my heart is not haughty, nor mine eyes lofty: neither do I exercise myself in great matters, or in things too high for me. Surely I have behaved and quieted myself, as a child that is weaned of his mother: my soul is even as a weaned child" (Ps. 131:1–2). In other words, David said, "I found out I had to grow up. I needed to get off milk and start eating porterhouse steak. I needed to eat of the Bread of Life." God tested David, and that testing enabled him to grow up. Paul wrote in the Book of Romans that patience is one of the results of being justified by faith: "And not only so, but we glory in tribulations also: knowing that tribulation worketh patience; And patience, experience; and experience, hope" (Rom. 5:3–4). There is a purpose in it all, you see.

There are many shallow and superficial saints today. There are many who are insecure as Christians. There are believers who try to be intellectual and who question the Word of God. And there are those who feel that as Christians we should try the "new morality." My friend, the problem with such believers is that they have never grown up—they are still little babes. God gives testing and trials to produce patience in our lives and that we might become full-grown children of God. How we need that today.

God must send us trouble so that we learn patience, which will also produce hope and love in the lives of men and women. Over the years of my ministry I have seen the Holy Spirit work this out in the lives of many folk. I recall one man who, when I first knew him, was always finding fault; as a pastor I had never had such a critic before. Then he began to attend the midweek Bible study at the church. I noticed that he brought his Bible and took notes. Over a period of ten years God sent that man a great deal of trouble, but he grew up and became one of the sweetest Christians I have ever known in my life. This is the type of testing which God gives to those who are His own.

> **If any of you lack wisdom, let him ask of God, that giveth to all men liberally, and upbraideth not; and it shall be given him [James 1:5].**

"Wisdom" here is related to the trials which James has been talking about. You and I have troubles and trials and problems. How are you going to solve this problem? How are you going to meet this issue? How are you going to deal with this person? If you lack wisdom in regard to a problem, you need to go to God in prayer.

Wisdom is the exercise and practical use of knowledge. Many people have knowledge, but they do not have any practical sense whatsoever. Even to this day I get a good laugh just thinking about the man with a Ph.D. with whom I used to play golf. One day out on the golf course it began to rain, and he looked at me in utter amazement and asked, "What shall we do now?" Well, you don't need a Ph.D. to know that you need to get in out of the rain! I said to him, "I think we'd better seek shelter." Wisdom is to know how to act under certain circumstances of testing, of trial, or when problems or questions arise. Life is filled with these, and you and I need wisdom from God.

"That giveth to all men liberally and upbraideth not." God is in the business of giving out wisdom "liberally," that is, simply. He will just simply help you out in times like that. He "upbraideth not" means, according to Marvin R. Vincent in his *Word Studies in the New Testament*, the "pure, simple giving of good without admixture of evil or bitterness." If we lack wisdom, let's go to God who will hear and answer our prayer.

> **But let him ask in faith, nothing wavering. For he that wavereth is like a wave of the sea driven with the wind and tossed [James 1:6].**

Maybe it is not your problem, but it has been my problem over a great deal of my Christian life that I simply have not believed God. Don't misunderstand me—I have trusted Christ as my Savior, and I believe with all my soul that He saved me and is going to save me for heaven. I believe that with all my heart, but down here in this life, where the rubber meets the road, is where I have had my problems. For example, I went through college in almost total unbelief—I didn't believe God could put me through college. I was a poor boy who had to borrow money and work at a full-time job. It was difficult. Every year I would finish, thinking I would not be able to come back the next year. Lo and behold, God always opened up a door, and I was able to continue. I was actually a miserable fellow as I went through college; when I look back, I realize I could have had a lot more fun if I had only believed God.

"But let him ask in faith nothing wavering." Why don't you believe God, my friend? Do you as a Christian have a long face today? Are you wondering how your problems are going to work out? I know exactly how you feel—I've been there. Why don't you believe God? Why don't you trust Him and turn them over to Him? I know I do not have the brains to meet the problems of life; I know I am not capable of living in this complex civilization, but I have a heavenly Father who can supply the wisdom that I need.

"For he that wavereth is like a wave of the sea driven with the wind and tossed." We say, "I believe God is going to work this out," but then we jump at it ourselves and make our own decision. So often I turn a problem over to the Lord and believe Him, but then the next day I do not believe Him. I decide that nothing has shown up by way of solution, so I will solve it myself. That's where I make my mistake. Such a man is "like a wave of the sea driven with the wind and tossed."

For let not that man think that he shall receive anything of the Lord [James 1:7].

If you are going to work out your problem for yourself, then God cannot work it out for you. Instead of going like a bull into a china closet and trying to work something out, why not turn it over to God?

Now James gives a proverb, and it is a good one—

A double-minded man is unstable in all his ways [James 1:8].

This was Israel's big problem. Hosea said Israel was like a silly dove. She first flew off to Egypt seeking help, and then she flew to Assyria. She turned first to one and then to the other, but she did not turn to God. Many times when a problem comes up we go here and there trying to solve it, until it occurs to us that we have never taken it to God. When you started out today did you turn the issues of the day over to God? I used to do a great deal of counseling as a pastor, and I would meet many new people during the day. One of the prayers I always prayed was, "Lord, I'm going to meet some new people today, and I don't know how to treat them. This man may prove to be a wonderful friend who wants to help me get out the Word of God. This other man may be seeking to hurt my ministry. Lord, help me to know the difference. Help me to be able to know which man I can put my arm around and help, and make me wary of the man who does not want my help at all. Lord, give me wisdom today." We need wisdom to meet the issues of life.

Let the brother of low degree rejoice in that he is exalted [James 1:9].

You may say, "I'm just a poor individual. I don't have very much. I don't have any wealth." My friend, if you are a child of God you have a lot of wealth. You have treasure in heaven. And have you ever stopped to think what you have down here, what you have in Christ? We have everything in Him. Paul wrote, "Therefore let no man glory in men. For all things are yours; Whether Paul, or Apollos, or Cephas, or the world, or life, or death, or things present, or things to come; all are yours; And ye are Christ's; and Christ is God's" (1 Cor 3:21–23). I belong to Christ, and everything He has He will make over to me. I have life. I have blessings. Even death is coming to me someday, if Christ doesn't come in the meantime. All of that is from Him, and all of these things we can rejoice in. It does not matter if you are the humblest saint or the poorest person on earth, you are rich in Christ, my friend, and you have something to rejoice over.

> **But the rich, in that he is made low: because as the flower of the grass he shall pass away [James 1:10].**

I always think of this verse when I walk across the campus of my alma mater. Every building there is named for some rich man. Do you know where those rich men are today? They are like the flowers which bloomed yesterday but are gone today. I think of how powerful they were, the riches and the influence they had, but today they are pushing up daisies somewhere and they have faded away. Don't rejoice in the fact that you are a rich man, because you will not have your money very long. You may have invested in gilt-edged bonds, and you may have stocks which you do not think you will lose. My friend, you may not lose them, but those stocks and bonds are going to lose you one of these days. In death you will not be able to hold on to them. The old adage says, "There's no pocket in a shroud." You won't be able to take it with you. The rich man is like the flower of the grass—he shall pass away.

> **For the sun is no sooner risen with a burning heat, but it withereth the grass, and the flower thereof falleth, and the grace of the fashion of it perisheth: so also shall the rich man fade away in his ways [James 1:11].**

I had the privilege years ago of speaking occasionally to a group of Christians in Hollywood, California. Among those who attended was a movie star who had become a Christian later on in life. She was getting old at that time, and when I looked at her I thought of how that beauty, which had brought her fame and fortune at one time, was now passing away. God says that the rich man shall "fade away in his ways."

My friend, rejoice today that you have a Savior who is not only going to save you for heaven—that's good enough for me—but He is going to help you this very day.

When I teach the Book of Proverbs I liken it to a young man who is considering the catalogs he has received from different universities— among which is the University of Wisdom. Here in the Epistle of James we find a different school—the School of Hard Knocks. That is the school most of us are in today. God wants to bring all those who are His own to full maturity as Christians, and He has many tests for doing that. He tests all of His children to see whether or not they are genuine, to weed out the phonies and the pseudosaints. He also wants to give assurance to His children. We should not regard our trials as evidence that we are not His children but rather as proof positive of our faith. My friend, if you are not having a little trouble today, you should question your salvation; if you are having trouble, that is a good sign that you belong to Him. While God has many goals in His testing, the one James has emphasized here is patience. God not only wants to give you proof that you are a genuine child of His, he also wants to produce patience in your life.

Much has been written about testing and God's purposes in it. William Penn, the man from whom the state of Pennsylvania got its name, made this statement: "No pain, no balm. No thorn, no throne. No gall, no glory. No cross, no crown."

Someone else has expressed it like this: "If I must carry a burden, Christ will carry me. Sometimes we must be laid low before we look high. In ourselves we are weak, even where we are strong. In Christ we are strong, even where we are weak. It's not how long you'll live, but how you are going to live." This perspective is important to have.

Many people wonder why in the world they must endure a particular experience. A number of years ago I received a letter from a Christian man who wrote: "I have a wife who has been sick for the past twenty years and has been paralyzed for the last ten years with Parkinson's disease. There is no hope of her ever leaving the hospital. How can a loving Father make a person suffer and linger as she has? And I know she loves the Lord." This man was genuinely concerned. He didn't have an answer for his problem, and neither did I. I couldn't tell him why it was happening, but I could tell him there was a purpose in it and that God was working out something in her life.

**Blessed is the man that endureth temptation: for when
he is tried, he shall receive the crown of life, which the
Lord hath promised to them that love him [James 1:12].**

"Temptation" is the same word as we have had before, which is sometimes translated as "testing" or "trying." "Temptation" is a good translation if you understand it in a good sense, as we will see later in this
chapter.

"Blessed is the man that endureth temptation: for when he is tried,
he shall receive the crown of life, which the Lord hath promised to
them that love him." Testing is one of God's methods of developing us
in the Christian faith. This is the way He is going to enable us to grow
and develop patience in our lives down here, but He also has something in mind for the future—"the crown of life."

Testing of any kind, but especially if it is a severe calamity or tragedy, has a tendency to produce a miasma of pessimism and hopeless-
ness. I do not blame the man whose wife was ill with Parkinson's
disease for feeling like he did. I do not blame him for asking, "Why?"
But the child of God can have the confidence that God is doing it for a
very definite reason and that He has a purpose in it all.

However, the man of the world will sink beneath the waves of adversity. Life, even at its best, makes him pessimistic. How many pessi-
mists are there today? How many cynics? How many are there who are
filled with bitterness, although they have everything? We are seeing an
epidemic of suicides among teenagers, and thousands of other young
people are dropping out of society today. Why? It is because they have
no goal in life. One of the more sensible news commentators made this
remark: "Back during the depression people had a will to live and
there were very few suicides, but today when everything has been
given to them they want to die."

When faith is tested and surrounded by darkness, when the waves
are rolling high and all seems lost, the child of God knows that this is
not the end. It may be gloom now, but it will be glory later on. As the
psalmist said, ". . . weeping may endure for a night, but joy cometh in

the morning" (Ps. 30:5). James says here, "He shall receive the crown
of life, which the Lord hath promised to them that love him."

I have noticed that people who have suffered a great deal have been
brought into a closer loving relationship with the Lord Jesus Christ.
Someone has expressed it like this:

> Is there no other way open, God,
> Except through sorrow, pain, and loss,
> To stamp Christ's likeness on my soul—
> No other way except the cross?
>
> And then a voice stills all my soul
> As stilled the waves of Galilee,
> "Can'st thou not bear the furnace heat
> If midst the flames I walk with thee?
>
> "I bore the cross. I know its weight.
> I drank the cup I hold for thee.
> Can'st thou not follow where I lead?
> I'll give thee strength. Lean hard on Me."
>   —Author unknown

You see, suffering brings an individual into a loving relationship
with Christ. And it causes him to look forward to that day when he
will be brought into the presence of the Lord Jesus who will give him
the crown of life.

What is "the crown of life"? There are many crowns mentioned in
Scripture which are given as *rewards* to believers. A crown is not salvation, but it represents a reward. It is something that is given to an
individual as a reward. For example, there was an unknown boy from
California who went to the Olympic Games and won six gold medals.
Suddenly his face was seen on every billboard, on television, and even
in commercials. I am told he also signed a movie contract. He won six
medals—he received his rewards. My Christian friend, the Lord Jesus
has a reward for those who will endure down here. James says, "He
shall receive the crown of life, which the Lord hath promised to them
that love him."

Testing will either drive you to the Lord or it will drive you away from Him. So many Christians become bitter. My friend, it is not going to be a pleasant experience to come someday into the presence of Christ if you have let the very thing your heavenly Father was using to develop your character and to bring you into a loving relationship with the Lord Jesus Christ make you bitter. We will have testings, but there is going to be a crown of life for those who persevere under trial.

I have done a great deal of reading about the crowns which are mentioned in Scripture, and I sometimes wonder where some of the interpreters get all their information. Let me give you my very simple interpretation of what I think a crown of life is. We find in Scripture that there are different kinds of punishment for the lost. Some will receive so many stripes; others will receive more stripes. There are *degrees of punishment* for the lost. Likewise there are *degrees of rewards* for believers. I do not expect to receive the reward that a man like Paul the apostle or Martin Luther or John Wesley will receive. Although I don't expect to receive a reward as they will, I do hope that I can come in for something—I am very much interested in that. I think that a "crown of life" is that which can bring you into a closer relationship with the Lord Jesus more than anything else possibly could.

In the Book of Revelation it speaks about the Lord giving to each of His own a stone with a name written on it (see Rev. 2:17). We have assumed that that means He will give each of us a new name. There's an old favorite gospel song that says, "There's a new name written down in glory. . . ." Well, it is not the new name spoken of in Revelation, but it is *your* name that is written down in glory if you are a child of God. As best as I can determine, the new name spoken of in Revelation means that God is going to give each of us a stone on which there is written a name of Christ which applies to our experience with Him. To you He means something a little special other than what He might mean to someone else. In other words, the Lord Jesus means something to you that He does not mean to me. He means something to me that He does not mean to you.

I can remember a time in my life as a young fellow that I stood at the crossroads at a Bible conference, trying to decide if I would go into the ministry or continue to follow a life of sin. There was a girl there at that conference in whom I was very much interested, but she was not really what you would call Bible conference material. I never shall forget that night yonder in Middle Tennessee. I crawled in under a water maple tree which was thick with leaves. In the shade—for the moon was shining brightly—I got down on my face and told the Lord Jesus that I needed His help and strength to make a decision. As a result of that night He means something to me that I'm sure He does not mean to you. You probably have a precious moment in your life which I have not experienced. I believe that the new name written on a stone is going to reflect what Christ means specially to you.

It is my conclusion that the crown of life means that you are going to have a degree of life in heaven which someone else will not have. There are a lot of folk who have gone through this world without doing anything for God. I thank God there was one thief on a cross who turned to Christ, but I cannot imagine that he will get very much of a reward, especially when I compare him to a man like Paul the apostle. Imagine what it is going to be like someday when Paul receives the crown of life!

Paul was very much interested in the crown of life, and James was interested in it too. There will be a crown of life, but you cannot receive that crown of life until you have been out on the racecourse of life, until you have gotten right down where the rubber meets the road and where life is being lived out. If you can live for God down here, my friend, He has a crown of life for you someday. That is something to which we can look forward.

When I think of the testings of this life, I am reminded of the deacon who got up in a testimony meeting in which the people were being asked to give their favorite verses of Scripture. This deacon got up and said, "My favorite verse is 'It came to pass.'" The minister looked up in amazement, and all the people were puzzled. Finally, the pastor asked, "Brother, what do you mean your favorite verse is 'It came to pass'?" The man replied, "When I have trouble and trials, I just go to the Lord and praise Him and say, 'I thank You, Lord, that it came to pass—it didn't come to stay!'" Thank God for that, my friend. I don't know a better way of putting it: The trouble hasn't come to stay.

James uses the same argument to warn the rich when he says, "You are like the grass and the flower of the grass." It may look pretty for you today. Life may be beautiful, my friend, but the flower is withering and your riches will not deliver you. Someday you will stand before Jesus Christ. Every human being is to stand before Him—the unbelievers will stand before God at the Great White Throne judgment. Also all believers, called the church, will go beforehand to the *bema* seat of Christ to see whether or not they will receive a crown of life. I don't know about you, but I'd like to have that crown, the crown which He offers to those who, after they have endured the testings of this life, love Him.

GOD DOES NOT TEST WITH EVIL

"Temptation" is used in two senses: testing under trial, as we have seen in verse 12, and now solicitation to evil, verses 13–14. James is now going to talk about that temptation, which is temptation to do evil. People often say that the Lord tested them when it wasn't the Lord at all. God cannot be tempted with evil, and He does not tempt with evil. James deals with something here which is very important for God's children to understand, because we often blame God for a great many things in our lives for which He is not responsible.

> **Let no man say when he is tempted, I am tempted of God: for God cannot be tempted with evil, neither tempteth he any man [James 1:13].**

We have seen in the preceding verses that God tests His own children, but now James makes it very clear that God never tests men with evil and with sin. "Let no man say when he is tempted, I am tempted of God"—a more literal translation is this: "Let not one man being tempted say, I am tempted of God." Notice that James is no longer using the noun temptation as he was previously. He is now using the verb; he is speaking of the action.

The natural propensity of mankind is to blame God for his own fumbles, all of his foibles, all of his faults and failures and filth. From the very beginning, since the time of the fall of man, this has been true. Adam said, ". . . The woman whom thou gavest to be with me, she gave me of the tree, and I did eat" (Gen. 3:12)—he really passed the buck! The woman did the same thing; she said, " . . . The serpent beguiled me . . ." (Gen.3:13). Actually, all three of them were responsible.

We often hear questions like this: Why does God send floods and earthquakes and allow the killing of babies? We blame God today for the result of the greed and avarice and selfishness of mankind—that is what is really responsible for floods and earthquakes. Man builds too close to a river and, when in the natural course of events the river rises, he calls it a flood and an act of God. But man thinks it is more pleasant to build by the river, or it's nearer transportation, or that is where the business is. It is actually the greed and avarice of man that causes him to build where it is really dangerous to build.

If you are going to live in Southern California, for example, you are going to take a chance on having an earthquake—you can be sure of that. We had a small one just the other evening as my wife and I were sitting in our den. The seismologists predict that we are in for a big earthquake here, yet people are still streaming into Southern California and putting up high-rise buildings. We ought not to blame God if a slab of concrete falls off one of those high-rise buildings and kills one of our loved ones. It would be much safer in the wide open spaces of Texas. I'm a Texan, but who wants to go back there? I know it's nicer there than when I was just a boy growing up, but I want to stay here in California. However, I'm not going to blame God when the earthquake comes. We have already been warned that it is coming.

Men also blame God in their philosophies today. Pantheism, for instance, says that everything is God, but good is God's right hand and evil is His left hand. Fatalism says that everything is running like blind necessity. If there is a God, they say, He has wound up this universe like an eight-day clock and has gone off and left it. Materialism's explanation of the problem with the human race is that the loftiest aspirations and the vilest passions are the natural metabolism of a physical organism.

God has answered these philosophies in His Word. There is no evil in God. In Him all is goodness and all is light and all is right. John wrote in his first epistle, "This then is the message which we have heard of him, and declare unto you, that God is light [that is, He is holy], and in him is no darkness at all" (1 John 1:5). The Lord Jesus made this very interesting statement: " . . . for the prince of this world cometh, and hath nothing in me" (John 14:30). That means there is no evil or sin in Him. But every time Satan gets around me, he is able to find something in me.

Let me introduce something which is theological at this point: *Jesus could not sin*. Someone will immediately ask, "Why, then, was He tempted?" In Matthew 4:7 our Lord said to Satan, " . . . It is written again, Thou shalt not tempt the Lord thy God." God wants to save from sin, and He does not tempt men to sin—He wants to deliver men. He never uses sin as a test, but He will permit it, as we shall see. The Lord Jesus had no sin in Him—"The prince of this world cometh, and hath nothing in me." The reason He was tempted was to prove that there was nothing in Him. After He had lived a life down here for thirty three years, Satan came with this temptation, a temptation that appealed to man's total personality—the physical side, the mental side, and the spiritual side of man. The Lord Jesus could not fall, and the testing was given to demonstrate that He could not fall. If He could have fallen, then any moment your salvation and mine is in doubt. The minute He yielded to sin, we would have no Savior. His temptation was to prove that He could not sin.

Let me illustrate this with a very homely illustration from my boyhood in west Texas. My dad built cotton gins for the Murray Gin Company, and we lived in a little town that was near a branch of the Brazos River. In the summertime there wasn't enough water in that river to rust a shingle nail, but when it began to rain in wintertime, you could almost float a battleship on it. One year a flood washed out the wooden bridge on which the Santa Fe railroad crossed the river. They replaced it with a steel bridge, and when they completed it, they brought in two locomotives, stopped them on top of the bridge, and tied down both of the whistles. All of us who lived in that little town knew for sure that something was happening. We ran down to see what it was—all twenty-three of us! When we got there, one of the braver citizens asked the engineer, "What are you doing?" The engineer replied, "Well, we built this bridge, and we are testing it." The man asked, "Why? Do you think it's going to fall down?" That engineer drew himself up to his full height and said, "Of course it will not fall down! We are *proving* it won't fall down." For the same reason, Jesus was tested to prove that you and I have a Savior who could not sin. God cannot be tempted with sin, and God will not tempt you with sin.

However, God does *permit* us to be tempted with sin. In 2 Samuel 24:1 we read, "And again the anger of the LORD was kindled against Israel, and he moved David against them to say, Go, number Israel and Judah." Frankly, that was sinful. Then, *did* God tempt David with evil? My friend, to understand the Bible you always need to get the full story. In 2 Samuel you have man's viewpoint of the events recorded. From man's viewpoint it looked as if God was angry with Israel and He simply had David do this. However, in 1 Chronicles we are told God's viewpoint of it: "And Satan stood up against Israel and provoked David to number Israel" (1 Chr 21:1). Who provoked David to sin? It was Satan, not God. God merely permitted Satan to do that because He was angry with Israel and their sin. God never tempts men with evil.

Who is responsible for our propensity to evil? What causes us to sin? Someone will say, "Well, you have just shown that it is Satan." Let's look at what James has to say in verse 14—

But every man is tempted, when he is drawn away of his own lust, and enticed [James 1:14].

We are talking here about the sins of the flesh. Who is responsible when you are drawn away to do evil? When you yield to evil temptation? God is not responsible. The Devil is not responsible. You are responsible.

A man got lost in the hills of Arkansas back in the days of the Model T Ford. He had lost his way, and there were no highway markings. He came into a small town and saw some little boys playing there. He asked one of them, "Where am I?" The little fellow looked at him puzzled for just a moment. Finally he pointed at the man with his finger and said, "*There* you are!" My friend, when you ask, "Who tempted me to do this?" God says, "*There* you are. It's in your own skin—that is where the problem is."

"Every man is tempted." *Every* man—this is the declaration of the individuality of the personality in the race of mankind. Just as each one of us has a different fingerprint, each one of us has a different moral nature. We have our own idiosyncrasies, our own eccentricities. All of us have something a little different.

One man was talking to another and said, "You know everybody has some peculiarity." "I disagree with you," said the other. "I don't think I have a peculiarity." "Well, then, let me ask you a question. Do you stir your coffee with your right hand or with your left hand?" asked the first man. "I stir it with my right hand," the other man replied. "Well, that's your peculiarity. Most people stir their coffee with a spoon!" May I say to you, all of us have our peculiarities. One person may be tempted to drink. Another may be tempted to overeat. Another may be tempted in the realm of sex. The problem is always within the individual. No outside thing or influence can make us sin. The trouble is here, within us, with that old nature that we have.

I think of the little boy who was playing around one evening in the pantry. He had gotten down the cookie jar. His mother called to him and said, "Willie, what are you doing in the pantry?" He said, "I'm fighting temptation!" He was in the wrong place to fight temptation, but that is the same place a lot of grown-up people are today. Many things are not bad within themselves, but it is the use we make of them that is wrong. Food is good, but you can become a glutton. Alcohol is medicine, but you can become an alcoholic if you abuse it. Sex is good if it is exercised within marriage. When it is exercised outside of marriage, you are going to experience several kinds of damage. Our society has an epidemic of venereal disease because of the looseness of the "new morality" today.

Many psychologists are trying to help us get rid of our guilt complexes. A Christian psychologist who taught in one of our universities here in Southern California told me one time, "You need to emphasize in your teaching that guilt complex more than you do. A guilt complex is as much a part of you as your right arm. You just cannot get rid of it."

However, the godless psychologist may attempt to remove the guilt complex in the wrong way. For example, a Christian lady called me one time and said, "Dr. McGee, a most frightful thing has happened to me. I've been having a real problem and have been on the verge of a nervous breakdown due to certain trials I've been going through. I went to a psychologist whom my doctor recommended. When he found out that I was a Christian, he said, 'What you need to do is to go downstairs to the barroom and pick up the first man you find there. Then you'll get rid of your guilt complex.'" I agree with the woman that such counsel is frightful indeed!

Then there are other psychologists who say, "What about your background? Did your mother love you? Did anything unusual happen while you were in the womb?" If you said, "Well my mother was caught in a rainstorm while she was carrying me," the psychologist would say, "That's the reason you're a drip!" Well, he *practically* says that when he blames his patient's problems on the mother.

My friend, you could solve a great deal of your problems for which you are blaming someone else if you would say to the living Lord Jesus who is right now at God's right hand, "I'm a sinner. *I'm* guilty." Then He will remove your guilt complex—He is the only One who can do that.

Proverbs says, "For as he [man] thinketh in his heart, so is he . . ." (Prov. 23:7). The solicitation to sin must have a corresponding response from within. James says that it is of your own lust (lust is an overweening desire and uncontrolled longing) that you are drawn away into sin. The Lord Jesus said, "I will draw all men unto Me" (see John 12:32), but the scoffer says, "He'll *not* draw me!" My friend, He will not force you. Hosea tells us that He will only use bands of love to draw us to Himself. He wants to woo and win you by His grace and love. Frankly, evil is attractive today; it is winsome. We are told that Moses was caught up at first in the pleasures of sin. Man can be enticed; the hook can be baited. If he yields, before long a person will become an alcoholic or a dope addict.

> **Then when lust hath conceived, it bringeth forth sin: and sin, when it is finished, bringeth forth death [James 1:15].**

In other words, when the desire of the soul, having conceived, gives birth to sin, the sin, having been completed, brings forth death. James uses a very interesting word here: "when lust hath *conceived*." The word actually means "to become pregnant." Conception is the joining or union of two. The desire of this old nature of ours joins with the outward temptation that faces us and thus becomes sin. The Lord Jesus said, "If you are angry with your brother, you are guilty of murder"—because it begins in the heart and moves out into action. He also said, "If you look upon a woman to lust after her, you have already committed adultery with her"—because it begins in your heart. That is where sin always begins.

The natural question at this point is: Is temptation sin? Of course it's not sin; the answer is definitely no. It is when the conception takes place—when the thought in the heart is carried out in action—that temptation becomes sin. Martin Luther expressed it in this novel way: "You cannot keep birds from flying over your head, but you can keep them from nesting in your hair." Sin is the consummation of the act inwardly and outwardly.

Temptation in and of itself is not sin. We all have an evil nature—there is no use trying to kid ourselves concerning that. We all have been tempted to do evil; everyone has a weakness in the flesh. One person may be a glutton and another may be a gossip. Both sins are absolutely of the flesh; both come from within. It is only the Lord Jesus who could say, " . . . for the prince of this world cometh, and hath nothing in me" (John 14:30).

"Then when lust hath conceived it bringeth forth sin." There cannot be a stillbirth. Lust is going to bring forth something. When that evil thought in the heart is joined to the outward temptation, there is a birth—a birth of the act, a birth of *sin*.

Now we rationalize sin today. We rationalize our bad tempers. We rationalize our gossip. We rationalize a lot of polite sins, and we even rationalize gross immorality; but the Bible calls them *sins*.

"And sin, when it is finished bringeth forth death." There are three kinds of death spoken of in Scripture. There is (1) *physical* death, and that comes to every man, you can be sure of that. Then there is (2) *spiritual* death, which is the condition of the lost man—he is "dead in trespasses and sins" (see Eph 2.1). Finally, there is (3) *eternal* death, which is the fate of the man who dies an unbeliever. The word *death* here primarily means "separation." Therefore, for a believer it means that when sin is born in his life, when it becomes an action, his fellowship with God is broken. There is a separation. In 1 John 1:6 we read, "If we say that we have fellowship with him, and walk in darkness, we lie, and do not the truth." You cannot have fellowship with Him and permit sin continually to happen in your life.

The great sin today, I suppose, is adultery. It is something that nearly every person has been faced with—and it is not something new. I think that the emphasis that is given to sex in our society and the present-day mode of dress have led to the committing of adultery probably more than it ever has been committed in American history. Certainly, adultery along with the free use of alcohol have pulled down the great nations of the past. Wine, women, and song have brought down the great nations of the world. Rome did not fall to some outside conqueror; Rome fell from within because it was honeycombed with sin. I recall a fine-looking young man who came to me and said, "I've fallen in love with a very beautiful girl. I want her to be mine." I asked him, "Have you asked her to marry you?" "Well, not exactly," he said. "She's married." I said, "You had better give up this notion right now." The young man went on to say, "But I want to ask you if it would be wrong for her to get a divorce and for us then to get married?" I told him, "Certainly it would be. You've been tempted, and I mean tempted a great deal, but as a child of God you would never be able to get by with such sin." I went on to tell him of several instances of couples who thought they could get by with it but were never happy.

It is tragic today when people think they can get by with sin. When lust conceives, it brings forth sin. The only kind of little brat that lust can bring into the world is sin, and sin will bring forth death. Sin will bring forth separation of fellowship with God if you are His child, and He will judge you for it unless you judge yourself.

That young man left my office after I had tried to put the fear of God in him. He was a wonderful Christian, and he surely had been tempted. He came back a few weeks later and said, "Dr. McGee, we have made our decision." I was certainly afraid they had made the wrong one, but he went on, "We recognize that in this life we never could be joined together. That's entirely out of the question for us. I'm simply asking God to let us be together someday in heaven." He worked with a very large company, and he told me that he had asked for a transfer to another city. I don't think a month went by before he came to me after the morning church service, shook my hand, and told me good-bye.

Temptation—there is a lot of it today. Many Christians say, "Oh, the Devil tempted me." My friend, temptation cannot conceive until it is joined with the desire of your evil nature. The important thing is that when it is joined, it will bring forth sin, and sin eventually brings forth death. If you are a child of God, it immediately breaks your fellowship with Him—and that is a death, by the way.

Do not err, my beloved brethren [James 1:16].

"Do not err"—the word here means to wander, to roam about, or to stray. It is like the little lost sheep the Lord Jesus told about which the shepherd went out after. James is saying, "Don't wander. Don't think that somehow you can get by with sin." The habitual and perpetual sinner definitely does not have a line of communication with God; he never has been born again. If you can live in sin and enjoy it, you are not a child of God—it's just that simple.

The story is told of the Calvinist and the Arminian who were having an argument. The Calvinist believes that once you are saved you can never be lost; the Arminian believes you can lose your salvation. The Arminian said, "If I believed your doctrine and were sure I was converted, I would take my fill of sin." To which the Calvinist replied, "How much sin do you think it would take to fill a genuine Christian to his own satisfaction?" May I say to you, that is a tremendous answer. If you can be satisfied with sin, you need to examine yourself to see whether or not you are in the faith. "He that falls into sin is a man," someone has said. "He that grieves at sin is a saint. He that boasts of sin is a devil." My friend, all of us are subject to temptation, but let's make sure that we do not give birth to sin. There can be no abortion here if you go through with temptation. Sin and death *will* be the end result.

Every good gift and every perfect gift is from above, and cometh down from the Father of lights, with whom is no variableness, neither shadow of turning [James 1:17].

One side of the moon is dark, and the other side is light. But in God there is no dark side. In all of us there is a shadow; you and I cast a shadow. The story is told that when Alexander the Great had conquered the world and returned to Greece, he looked up his old teacher, Aristotle, to tell him all that had happened. When he found Aristotle, he was taking a bath. Alexander stood in the doorway and told Aristotle what had happened. Then he said, "Now I am prepared to give you anything in the world that you want. What do you want?" Aristotle looked up and replied, "I want you to get out of my light!" May I say to you, that's all any of us do—we cast a shadow. But there is no shadow in God at all.

"With whom is no variableness." God doesn't vary; He doesn't change, as the laws of creation reveal. God is not on a yo-yo like a lot of Christians are today—up today and down tomorrow, and round and round they go.

"Every good gift and every perfect gift is from above." I have a friend who is an insurance agent, and I like to kid him about the wording in his house insurance policy. It says that the policy does not include certain things which might happen to your house, including "any act of God." I said to him "What in the world do you think God is going to do to my house?" "Well," he said, "there could be a cyclone or something like that." I asked, "Do you think God is to be blamed for that?" I realize that it is just an expression which is used, but it has been the custom down through the centuries to blame God for such things. My friend, if you have a good gift, it came from Him. Count your many blessings today: the sunshine, the rain, the cloudy day, the bright day, the green grass, the water you drink, and the air you breathe. God gave us clean air and pure water. It is man who has polluted it. God gives *good* gifts, my friend. God is good! You and I don't really understand how good He is.

Of his own will begat he us with the word of truth, that

we should be a kind of firstfruits of his creatures [James 1:18].

This is definitely a reference to the new birth. How does He beget us? "With the word of truth, that we should be a kind of firstfruits of his creatures." *Beget* means "to bring forth." There are those who say, "Well, if I am predestined to be lost, there is nothing I can do about it. And if I am to be saved, I'll be saved." There are two wills involved here—"Of his own will begat he us." Again, you have in conception *two* coming together—there is no other way for a conception to take place. Therefore, when His will is joined with your will, you will be born again. Don't tell me that you are not responsible. It is not His will that any should perish. You are begotten by the Word of God. When you are willing to come, when you believe the Word of God and accept Jesus Christ as your Savior, you will be born again. "Being born again, not of corruptible seed, but of incorruptible, by the word of God, which liveth and abideth for ever" (1 Pet. 1:23).

Wherefore, my beloved brethren, let every man be swift to hear, slow to speak, slow to wrath [James 1:19].

"Wherefore, my beloved brethren"—James is talking to the child of God.

"Let every man be swift to hear." Swift to hear what? To hear the Word of God, of course. After you have been begotten by the Word of God, you are not through with it. You are going to *grow* by the Word of God. You have something that is living, powerful, and sharper than any two-edged sword (see Heb. 4:12)."But the natural man receiveth not the things of the Spirit of God: for they are foolishness unto him: neither can he know them, because they are spiritually discerned" (1 Cor. 2:14). However, as a child of God you are indwelt by the Spirit of God who wants to teach you the Word of God. The Creator of this universe and the Redeemer of lost sinners wants to talk to you, my friend. James says, "Be swift to hear. Be alert." As I stand before a church congregation, I sometimes feel like crying out to them, "Wake up!" or, "The place is on fire!" because I would like to get them alert and moving. Oh, how we need to be alert and quick to hear the Word of God.

"Slow to speak." God gave us *two* ears and *one* mouth—there must be a very definite reason for that. There is a real danger of our talking too much. There are those who argue that the minute someone is saved they should begin to witness. I do not think a newborn Christian is quite ready to witness. If he got saved last night, we want to hear his testimony today—especially if he is a prominent person, if he is a rich man, if he has been a gangster, if he is in the entertainment business, or if he happens to be an outstanding politician. Those are the ones whose testimonies we are eager to hear. I often regret it when singers give a little talk before they begin their song. Many times I have just bowed my head in embarrassment at some of the things they have said. One sweet little girl had a lovely voice, but when she got up and said, "I've just been saved two months," I cringed, and I had a right to, because what she went on to say was as contrary to the Word of God as anything possibly could be. I also think it is a tragedy that some of these Hollywood entertainers have been encouraged to testify shortly after their salvation experience simply because they are well-known persons. Their theology is sometimes as rank as it can be. They need to study and know the Word of God before they are pushed up front to speak. God says we are to be quick to hear but slow to speak.

Someone will ask, "But aren't we to witness?" Yes, but be very careful how you witness and make sure about your own life first. The story is told about Socrates and a young man who was brought to him to enter his school. Socrates was a school teacher as well as a philosopher. The young man came in and was introduced to Socrates. Before he could say a word, the young man started talking, and he talked for about ten minutes. Finally, when the young man finished, Socrates said, "I'll take you as a student, but I'm going to charge you twice as much." The young man asked, "Why are you going to charge me double?" Socrates' reply was this: "First, I am going to have to teach you how to hold your tongue and then how to use it." James says, "Quick to hear but slow to speak." Christians need to be very careful not to reveal their ignorance of the Word of God. *Listen* to Him. Yes, the Bible says,

"Let the redeemed of the Lord say so," but we need to be very careful what we say.

"Slow to wrath"—that is, slow to anger. Don't argue about religion and lose your temper. It is good to be a fundamentalist, but don't start fighting about every little jot and tittle of theology with everybody in sight who disagrees with you. After all, you don't have *all* the truth.

Be "slow to wrath." Don't get angry. Jonathan Edwards was the third president of Princeton and probably one of America's greatest thinkers and preachers, but he had a daughter who had an uncontrollable temper. One day a fine young man at the school, who had fallen in love with her, came to Jonathan Edwards and asked for her hand in marriage. (That was the custom in that day, but it seems to have fallen by the wayside now.) Jonathan Edwards said, "You can't have her." The young man said, "But I love her." Edwards said, "You can't have her." The young man said, "But she loves me." Again Edwards said, "You can't have her." "Why can't I have her?" he protested. "Because she is not worthy of you," replied Jonathan Edwards. "Yes, she *is* a Christian, but the grace of God can live with some people with whom no one else could ever live." May I say to you, there are a lot of unworthy Christians today with uncontrollable tempers that spoil their testimonies as much as anything in this life can spoil them.

For the wrath of man worketh not the righteousness of God [James 1:20].

The anger of man is contrary to the will and work of God. This is the reason we shouldn't argue about religion. I have never yet found anybody who agrees with me 100 percent or with whom I agree 100 percent, but that is no reason for me to fall out with him. Someone came to my office the other day while I was listening to our broadcast as it came over the radio. He said to me, "What are you doing?" And I said to him, "You know, I am listening to the only man with whom I agree 100 percent!"

James says, "The wrath of man worketh not the righteousness of God." You may feel that you are angry because you are a defender of the faith, but, my friend, the wrath of man simply does not work the righteousness of God. Don't kid yourself that you are angry for His sake, because He's not angry—He's in the saving business.

> **Wherefore lay apart all filthiness and superfluity of naughtiness, and receive with meekness the engrafted word, which is able to save your souls [James 1:21].**

"Wherefore lay apart all filthiness"—that is, put away all filthiness of the flesh. "And superfluity of naughtiness" is better translated as "abundance of wickedness."

"And receive with meekness the engrafted word." The word *engrafted* should be "implanted"—the implanted Word of God. In other words, you are to receive the Word of God. I believe the Word of God is the greatest preventative against the sins of the flesh. The old Scottish preacher said, "Sin will keep you from the Bible, or the Bible will keep you from sin." He was certainly accurate in that.

"Which is able to save your souls." James is speaking to those who have been saved. You have received the implanted Word—it has been planted in your hearts. The Word has already brought salvation to you, but you have a life to live as a Christian. Salvation is in three tenses: I have been saved; I am being saved; I shall be saved. James is speaking here of salvation in the present tense.

GOD TESTS FAITH BY THE WORD, NOT BY MAN'S WORDS

The child of God can never get away from the Word of God. Every child wants to hear the voice of his father, especially if it is a voice of comfort as well as a voice of correction. One who isn't interested in the Word of God or doesn't stay near it—if he *is* a child of God—is going to get into trouble.

For a great many people this is the most familiar verse in the Epistle of James—

> **But be ye doers of the word, and not hearers only, deceiving your own selves [James 1:22].**

You and I live in a day when we have many translations of the Bible. They are multiplying—every year, two or three new translations are published. Personally, I have not found a new translation that I feel is really adequate to take the place of the Authorized Version. I think the Authorized Version needs improving in certain places, but I still use it, as you well know. However, we do need a new translation! It should be different from Tyndale's and from the Authorized Version and from the American Standard and from all of these new translations. Any Christian could make this new translation. You could make a new translation of the Bible. You might say, "You don't know me. I'm not capable—I'm not familiar with the original languages, and I know nothing about the handling of manuscripts." My friend, in spite of your limitations—which may be many—it is still possible for you to make the best translation of Scripture that has ever been made. Do you know what the name of that translation is? It is known as the Doer's Translation. "Be ye doers of the word." That's a good translation— a Doer's Translation.

Paul put the same thought in just a little different phraseology: "Ye are our epistle written in our hearts, known and read of all men: Forasmuch as ye are manifestly declared to be the epistle of Christ ministered by us, written not with ink, but with the Spirit of the living God; not in tables of stone, but in fleshy tables of the heart" (2 Cor. 3:2–3). The world today is not reading the Bible, but they are reading you and me. Someone has expressed it poetically:

> The Gospel is written a chapter a day
> By deeds that you do and by words that you say
> Men read what you say, whether faithless or true.
> Say, what is the Gospel according to you?

In verses 22 through 25 we have come to the real pragmatism of James. I like to outline these verses like this: (1) Verse 22—the *demands* of the Word; (2) verses 23–24—the *danger* of the Word; and (3) verse 25—the *design* of the Word. We have in this section that which is substantive, that which really gets down to where we live.

Here in verse 22 we have the *demands*, or the imperatives, of the

Word: "But be ye doers of the word, and not hearers only, deceiving your own selves." There is an element about the Word of God which makes it different from any other book. There are many books which you can read to gain information, knowledge, intellectual stimulation, spiritual inspiration, amusement, or entertainment. But the Word of God is different, and this is probably the reason it is not as popular as other books: it *demands action.* "Be ye *doers* of the word, and not hearers only." It requires attention. The Lord Jesus said, "If any man will *do* his will, he shall know of the doctrine, whether it be of God, or whether I speak of myself" (John 7:17, italics mine). The Word of God demands action: "O *taste* and see that the LORD is good . . . (Ps. 34:8, italics mine).

You can read history, but it asks nothing of you. You can read literature, but there are no imperatives, no declarations, and no explanations, although it may have a lesson to teach which may or may not have been in the mind of the author. You can read science, but it makes no demands on you whatsoever. You can read a cookbook and it gives you a recipe, but it does not say you have to cook. There is no demand that you mix up a batch of biscuits or that you make a chocolate cake. However, the Word of God is a command. It is a trumpet. It is an appeal for action. "He that believeth on the Son hath everlasting life: and he that believeth not the Son shall not see life; but the wrath of God abideth on him" (John 3:36). The message of the Lord Jesus Christ is (1) "repent"; (2) "come unto Me": and (3) "believe" (see Matt. 11:28; Mark 1:15). The Word of God demands belief.

All advertising today is high-pressured. It is being used on radio, television, billboards, and in newspapers and magazines. They all use the hard sell. We are not only being brainwashed by the news on television and radio, we are also being brainwashed by advertising. Madison Avenue is throwing everything at the consumer. You are to buy a certain make of car, and you are told how wonderful it is over last year's model—when about all they did was to make the steering wheel a little smaller than last year's. And you are told if you don't use a certain deodorant you will lose your job. But the Word of God says that you are going to die in your sins if you don't turn to Christ! Talk about high pressure—that is high pressure! The Word of God says, ". . . behold *now* is the accepted time . . ." (2 Cor. 6:2, italics mine), and, " . . . *Today* if ye will hear his voice" (Ps. 95:7, italics mine).

I believe that the greatest failure of the Christian church in recent years has been at this point. After World War II the Western world came out of the bomb shelters and went to church—prompted by fear of the bombs but not by fear of God. Church membership and attendance soared to new heights. I am very thankful I had a ministry during that period. I had a full church, and it was to me a glorious, wonderful time for ministry. But at that same time, lawlessness and immorality increased dramatically. Drunkenness, divorce, and juvenile delinquency escalated. And in the lives of Christians there was a total breakdown in separation from the things of the world. What had happened? The church had been getting out the Word of God in the passive voice; it had been giving it out in the subjunctive mood, but God had originally given it in the *imperative* mood. We had forgotten that a leather-bound Bible needs some shoe leather to go with it. Memorizing Scripture is good, but it also demands action.

"But *be ye* doers of the word." James does not use the ordinary Greek verb for "be," which is *eimi*; the word here is *ginesthe* which literally means "to become, to be born, to come into existence." The imperative given here is for the born-again child of God. God is not asking the unsaved person to do anything, except one thing—and that is actually not *doing*, but believing. When the people came to the Lord Jesus and asked, "What shall we do that we might inherit eternal life?" He replied, "Do? Why, this is the will of God that ye *believe* on Him whom He has sent" (see John 6:28–29). *Doing*, as far as God's will is concerned, for the unsaved is *believing* on Christ. God is not asking the unsaved to do anything at all; He wants to tell them that *He* has done something.

As a boy I played baseball on the school lot on Saturdays. I played first base, and it was a wonderful thing to which I really looked forward. We played the teams of other high schools around us, and it generally ended up in a fight no matter who we played. One Saturday as I was playing ball, I saw my dad coming up, and I knew he wasn't coming to see the game. He had come to tell me he had some work for me to do. The truth is, I had neglected taking care of my chores before I had left home. My dad didn't ask any of the other boys to do a single thing—he just asked me. Why? Those other boys weren't his sons; I was.

My friend, God isn't asking anything of you until you become His child. But to those of us who have become children of God, He says, "Be ye doers of the word and not hearers only, deceiving your own selves."

It is sometimes difficult for us preachers to see that we also need to be doers of the Word. I remember one time playing golf with a medical doctor friend who is also a wonderful Christian. Another friend of this doctor wanted to join us, so the doctor introduced me to his friend, saying, "This is Dr. McGee." The man said, "Oh, we have two doctors." I wanted to make it clear to him what kind of doctor I was, so I said, "I'm a doctor who *preaches*, and he's a doctor who *practices*." May I say, we need more Th.D.'s who practice as well as preach!

Someone expressed it in a little poem like this:

> It's easier to preach than to practice;
> It's easier to say than to do.
> Most sermons are heard by the many,
> But taken to heart by the few.
> —Author unknown

Hearing the Word of God will lead to doing by those who are His children. It will not lead to rote and ritual and habitual action; it will not lead to the drab, the monotonous, or the routine. The intent of the Word is to produce creative action and to make for productive performance, exciting living, and a thrilling experience. If we are motivated by an inner desire and are enjoying Spirit-filled living, you and I can go out on the golf course and enjoy playing golf and then enjoy Bible study equally as well—in fact, it will be thrilling to us.

Hearing the Word will lead to doing for God that which is motivated by an inner desire. As we began our radio broadcast ministry, we also began to build up our office staff. I know that it is the finest staff I have ever had in all my years of ministry. God has sent each individual

to us, and each has made a marvelous contribution. They are creative
and dedicated workers. It is my feeling that in God's work we need that
which is creative, that which is dynamic, that which produces.

"And not hearers only." There is a difference between being a student in a class and being an auditor. I used to have quite a few folk who
would audit my classes when I was teaching at the Bible Institute in
downtown Los Angeles many years ago. I had more trouble with the
auditors than I ever did with the students. They were constantly telling
me I was too hard on the students. They didn't realize I needed to be
hard-boiled, but the students understood that I was kidding them half
the time. Those auditors never had to take exams; they never had to
make preparation; they never wrote any papers; they never got a di-
ploma. They didn't do anything. They just sat there. Faith leads to
action, my friend—it will make you more than an auditor.

The story is told of a man who was always talking about his faith—
he never did anything for anybody; he just talked about his faith. One
day a friend came along and saw him stuck in the mud with his wagon.
The friend said, "Well, you sure are well established in the faith!" May
I say to you, what we need to do today is to keep moving. After we get
established, we need to keep moving in the faith and not get stuck in
the mud.

"Deceiving your own selves." Self-deception is a terrible thing.
The apostle John says that those who say they don't have any sin in
their lives do not deceive anyone but themselves (see 1 John 1:8). It is
very easy to fall into the trap of rationalizing our sin and rationalizing
our inaction.

In verses 23 and 24 we have the *danger* of the Word—

> **For if any be a hearer of the word, and not a doer, he is
> like unto a man beholding his natural face in a glass
> [James 1:23].**

"A man beholding his natural face in a glass." A very highly polished
piece of brass was used as a mirror in that day. A mirror is a very interesting thing, and it is used here as a picture of the Word of God. When
you look into a mirror, you see a reflection of yourself—you see yourself as you really are.

You may have noticed that on some pictures of Abraham Lincoln there is a wart on his cheek but that on others it is not there. As one artist was preparing to paint his portrait, he began to have Lincoln move around. He said, "President Lincoln, will you sit here?" Then this man would move his easel and have Lincoln shift around again. President Lincoln began to smile because he saw what the artist was doing. He was trying to get Lincoln in a position where the wart would not show. Finally the artist was satisfied, and he asked, "President Lincoln, how do you want me to paint you?" Lincoln replied, "Paint me just as I am—wart and all." That's what a mirror would tell you; if you have a wart, it will show up. That is one reason many of us don't like to spend too much time in the presence of a mirror. My friend, the Word of God will tell you what you are.

"For if any be a hearer of the word and not a doer, he is like unto a *man* beholding his natural face in a glass." Someone will say, "It ought to say *woman*." A woman usually carries a little mirror around with her to be sure her hair and makeup are all right. But what about men? Do they look in mirrors? They are just as vain, my friend. A man likes to be sure his tie is straight and his hair is combed. We are living in a day when our appearance seems to be very important. A mirror reveals our flaws.

There is a danger, though, of looking into the mirror, seeing the flaw but doing nothing about it.

For he beholdeth himself, and goeth his way, and straightway forgetteth what manner of man he was [James 1:24].

James is answering what he has said in verse 19 where he wrote, "Be swift to hear, slow to speak." Here his emphasis is, "Don't be so quick or hasty as you look into the mirror." The thought in being "swift to hear" is to give it all your attention, to be alert to the Word of God. What James is saying here is, "Don't treat it casually. Don't go over it hurriedly like that." Any man who is just a hearer of the Word and not a doer—his knowledge of the Bible doesn't lead to action—is like a man beholding his natural face in a mirror, "for he beholdeth himself, and goeth his way, and straightway forgetteth what manner of man he was."

Folk who do not like to read in the Bible the fact that they are sinners simply pass over those sections. That is the reason, I think, that textual preaching is outmoded. I feel that we need to go through the entire Word of God and not pull out nice, sweet verses here and there. God did not give His Word in verses; verses are man-made. We need to take the Word of God as it is. The Word is a mirror that reveals what is wrong with you. A man who goes to the doctor and has an X-ray taken which reveals a cancer in his body can respond by saying, "Now, look, doctor, I don't put much confidence in X-rays. I think I'll just ignore it and forget it." I've known some people who have said that, and they have died. When the doctor told me that I had cancer, I wanted treatment just as quickly as I could get it. My friend, you cannot afford to read the Word of God and not respond to it. It demands your response; and if you don't respond, *you* are responsible. If the doctor tells you you have cancer and you don't do anything about it, is the doctor responsible? He absolutely is not responsible at all. God has given you His Word, and you are responsible for your response to it. To a man who has been born again, the Word will say, "Look, you are no longer growing. You are actually leaving your first love." God uses His Word to remind us of Himself and to call us back.

One time I heard a song leader down in Chattanooga, Tennessee, say, "Let's stand and sing 'Standing on the Promises,' but the trouble is that we sing 'Standing on the Promises' when we are really sitting on the premises." That is what James is telling us not to do. The Word of God is a mirror which reveals our shortcomings, and we are not to forget what it says. "For the word of God is quick, and powerful, and sharper than any two-edged sword, piercing even to the dividing asunder of soul and spirit, and of the joints and marrow, and is a discerner of the thoughts and intents of the heart" (Heb. 4:12). The Word reveals us as we are, penetrating below the surface of our beings.

The Bible is not a popular book today. It is the best seller but the worst read. It is not popular because it shows us who we are. Many years ago in eastern Tennessee the story went around about a mountaineer's contact with some tourists who had camped in the hills around his area. Because the mountain folk didn't see many tourists in those days, when the tourists left, this particular mountaineer went to look around the area where they had camped. He found several things they had left behind, including a mirror. He had never seen a mirror before. He looked into it longingly and said, "I never knew my pappy had his picture took!" He was very sentimental about it, of course, and took it home. He slipped into the house, climbed up into the loft and hid the mirror. His wife saw him do that but didn't say anything. After he went out of the house, she went up to see what he had hidden. She found the mirror, and when she looked into it, she said, "So that's the old hag he's been running around with!" May I say to you, it is so easy to read the Word of God and to think it is a picture of someone else. It is a picture of you, and it is a picture of me.

In verse 25 we see the design of the Word—

> **But whoso looketh into the perfect law of liberty, and continueth therein, he being not a forgetful hearer, but a doer of the work, this man shall be blessed in his deed [James 1:25].**

Looketh means "to look attentively, penetratingly."

"The perfect law of liberty." This is not the Mosaic Law; it is the law of grace. James does not talk about law here in the same sense that Paul does. When Paul talks about law, he is talking about the Mosaic Law. When James talks about law, it is the law of faith. There is love in law in the Old Testament, and there is law in love in the New Testament. "If the Son therefore shall make you free, ye shall be free indeed" (John 8:36). However, the Lord also said, "If ye love me, keep my commandments" (John 14:15), and Paul said, "Bear ye one another's burdens, and so fulfil the law of Christ" (Gal. 6:2). What law? Christ's law. John says in his first epistle, "For this is the love of God, that we keep his commandments . . ." (1 John 5:3).

When you are driving down a freeway, you will see that it is loaded with traffic, and it is also loaded with laws. If you want to have freedom to drive down that freeway, you had better obey the laws. There is liberty in Christ, and it is the only true freedom. However, you can be sure that if you are in Christ, you are going to obey Him—and His laws are not hard; they are not rigorous. Because you are a child of God, your freedom does not entitle you to break the Ten Commandments. Those laws are for the weak, for the natural man. Laws are for law-breakers: what to do, where to go, and how, with a punishment prescribed for those who break over. Honest citizens do not need the law. I do not know one half of the laws of this state in which I live, but every shyster lawyer knows them, because he is seeking loopholes to break those laws.

Today God has called His children to a higher level. A child of God has a spiritual spontaneity, a high and lofty motive, an inspiration of God. The believer has no desire to murder. He lives above the law. He is now motivated by the love of the Savior, and he desires to obey Him. The more we read and study the Word, the more we will learn, we will love, and we will live. Joy fills and floods the soul. We are not like galley slaves, whipped and chained to a bench and doing that which we do not want to do.

You and I may not need to know all the laws of our state or of our country, but we certainly need to know the Word of God if we are to live for Him. I do not agree with the popular song today which says, "You don't need to understand, you just need to hold His hand." My friend, you *do* need to understand. You're not apt to be holding His hand unless you do understand. There are too many folk today who are ignorant of the Word of God. It is no disgrace to be ignorant. I don't know about you, but I was born ignorant. I didn't know A from B when I was born. I couldn't even walk or talk. I was in bad shape, but I didn't stay in that shape and neither did you. It's no disgrace to be ignorant, but it's a disgrace to stay ignorant if you are a child of God.

> **If any man among you seem to be religious, and bridleth not his tongue, but deceiveth his own heart, this man's religion is vain [James 1:26].**

Religious and *religion* are not actually Bible words—that is, they occur only about half a dozen times in the New Testament. James uses them more than any other New Testament writer. The word *religion* comes from a Latin word which means "to bind back." Although Herodotus used the word, it was not a word used commonly in the Greek language. He spoke of the *religion* of the Egyptian priests. The word has to do with going through a ritual, a form, or a ceremony.

There are many religions today, and they can demonstrate that they have faithful, zealous followers. But you cannot call a religion Christian simply because it conforms to certain outward forms of ritual. Christianity is not a religion; it is a person, and that person is Jesus Christ—you either have Him or you don't have Him.

James is saying here that if a religious man does not control his speech, his religion—regardless of what it is—is vain. What about the Christian and his tongue? James is going to have a great deal to say in chapter 3 about the child of God and this matter of bridling the tongue. Someone has said, "You can't believe half of what you hear, but you can repeat it." That is a real problem in the church today. We have too many people who have unbridled tongues.

> **Pure religion and undefiled before God and the Father is this, To visit the fatherless and widows in their affliction, and to keep himself unspotted from the world [James 1:27].**

This is a tremendous statement. "Pure" is the positive side, and "undefiled" is the negative side. You need to have both if you are to have the right kind of religion—and Christianity certainly ought to produce this.

"To visit the fatherless and widows in their affliction." This is the positive side. A child of God ought to be in personal contact with the sorrow of the world and the problems of the people of the world. This is where the politicians are very clever. They go out and meet the people and shake their hands. They make a personal contact. In the same way, Christians should be getting out where the people are. I feel there is a grave danger in our having a religion of the sanctuary but not a religion of the street. We need a religion of the street also. We should be in contact with the world in a personal way, with tenderness and kindness and helpfulness.

"And to keep himself unspotted from the world." This now is the negative side. Contact with the world does not mean that we should become implicated in the things of the world. As believers we are in this world but we are not *of* this world.

I think of the story of the little boy whose mother had died. His father was a poor man, but he worked and tried to raise the little fellow. There was a wealthy couple, relatives, who became interested in the boy. They said to the father, "You are not able to give the boy everything in life. We are wealthy; we can give him everything." So the father went to the little boy to talk to him about going to live with these folks. He said to the little fellow, "They'll give you a bicycle, give you toys, and give you wonderful gifts at Christmas. And they will take you on trips. They will do things for you that I can't do for you." The little boy said, "I don't want to go." And the father said, "Why?" The boy said, "They can't give me *you*." That's what the little fellow wanted. There are a lot of people out yonder today who want that personal contact. My friend, you can bring a Christian contact to these people with sweetness and love and consideration and kindness. But let us remember to keep ourselves unspotted from the world. We can get so implicated in the things of the world that it becomes a dangerous thing.

CHAPTER 2

THEME: God tests faith by attitude and action in re-spect of persons; God tests faith by good works

GOD TESTS FAITH BY ATTITUDE AND ACTION IN RESPECT OF PERSONS

In the first thirteen verses of this chapter, James is going to deal with how we are to treat people in the different strata of society. How do you treat the rich man? How do you treat the poor man? How do you treat the average man whom you meet today? This section deals with God's war on poverty and, interestingly enough, also God's war on riches. This is God's war on poverty and riches. His war on poverty is a little different from that of our government; no matter which political party has been in office, neither the federal nor the state governments have been able to deal successfully with this problem.

Both poverty and riches can be a curse. Part of the curse on the human race is poverty and riches. The writer in the Book of Proverbs says, ". . . give me neither poverty nor riches . . ." (Prov. 30:8). The most difficult people to reach are those who are the most poverty-stricken and those who are the richest; it seems to be almost impossible to reach either class with the Word of God.

The real problem is actually the imbalance of wealth in the world. The problem today is not between political parties, and it is not even between the races. The problem in the world is the imbalance of wealth. Take, for example, the nation of India where it is estimated there will soon be a population of one billion. There is great famine and starvation in that land; they starve by the thousands over there. Contrast that with the luxury and abundance which the wealthy have to-day. God goes after this problem in this epistle. He is on the side of the poor—I'm very delighted to say that. After all, when the Lord Jesus came into the world, He wasn't a rich man's boy; He wasn't born with a silver spoon in His mouth. He was born in poverty. He was born in a borrowed stable. He had to borrow loaves and fishes from a little lad to feed the crowd. He spoke from a borrowed boat. He said, "The foxes have holes, and the birds of the air have nests; but the Son of man hath not where to lay his head" (see Matt. 8:20). He had to borrow a coin to illustrate a truth. He borrowed a donkey to ride into Jerusalem. He borrowed a room to celebrate the Passover. He died on a borrowed cross—it belonged to Barabbas, not to Him. They put Him in a borrowed tomb—it belonged to Joseph of Arimathaea.

When I was in college, we had a preacher who came and talked about "the blessings of poverty." Now I was a poor boy, and I mean poor, my friend. I was going to school on borrowed money and was working full time. That man spoke every morning in chapel, and I was told that he got $15,000 a year (that was back in the days when a dollar was worth a dollar). It was a lot of money for a preacher in that day. You know, what he had to say just ran off my mind like water off a duck's back—he had no message for me. The blessings of poverty? I just happen to know, since I was born that way and haven't gotten too far from it yet, that there are no blessings in poverty. Poverty is a curse, and part of the curse which Christ bore was poverty.

Riches can also be a curse, as James will show in this epistle. Paul said, "For the love of money is the root of all evil . . ." (1 Tim. 6:10). Paul and James certainly agree here. You can spend your money for the wrong items. You can deposit your money in the wrong bank. "Lay not up for yourselves treasures upon earth, where moth and rust doth corrupt, and where thieves break through and steal" (Matt. 6:19). All the banks are telling us where to put our money, but God says, in effect, "I've got a bank, and I will keep investments up there for you." James will be harsh with the rich as we will see in chapter 5. Proverbs 30:8 should be the philosophy of every Christian: "Give me neither poverty nor riches."

What is God's solution to the problem of poverty? It is not to rob the rich in order to take care of the indigent, the lazy, the indolent, the drones, the loafers, the sluggards, and the laggards. On the other hand, God would never destroy the dignity and the self-respect and the integrity and the honor of the poor by placing them on charity. God's war on poverty and riches does not march under the banner of the dollar where millions are appropriated for relief. And it is not aimed primarily at the head or at the stomach, but at the heart. It is a war against class. James is talking about distinctions and divisions among believers which have been brought about by money.

My brethren, have not the faith of our Lord Jesus Christ, the Lord of glory, with respect of persons [James 2:1].

"*Have* not the faith of our Lord Jesus Christ" should be "*Hold* not the faith of our Lord Jesus Christ." Notice that James is His half brother according to the flesh, but he gives Him here the full name, "our Lord Jesus Christ." And he calls Him "the Lord of glory." Here is a strong assertion of the deity of Christ. I know of no one who was in a better position to determine the deity of Christ than a younger brother of the Lord Jesus who was brought up in the same home with Him. Frankly, I think James is in a better position to speak on the deity of Christ than some theologian sitting in a swivel chair in a musty library in New York City, removed from the reality of even his own day. Such a man is really far removed from the reality of the first century and the home in which Jesus was raised. Therefore, I go along with James, if you don't mind. He is the "Lord Jesus Christ, the Lord of glory."

What James is telling us here is not to profess faith in Christ and at the same time be a spiritual snob. Don't join some little clique in the church. *All* believers are brethren in the body of Christ, whatever their denomination. There is a fellowship of believers; friendship should be over them as a banner. James is addressing the total community of believers—the rich, the poor, the common people, the high, the low, the bond and free, the Jew and the Gentile, the Greek and the barbarian, male and female. They are all *one* when they are in the body of Christ. There is a brotherhood within the body of believers, and the Lord Jesus Christ is the common denominator. Friendship and fellowship are the legal tender among believers.

James says, "Don't hold your faith with respect of persons." If you belong to the Lord Jesus Christ and another person belongs to the Lord Jesus Christ, he is your brother. Furthermore, if a sinner comes into your assembly or you otherwise come into contact with him, remember that he is a human being for whom Christ died. He stands at the foot of the cross, just as you stand at the foot of the cross.

The Old Testament taught Israel not to regard the person of the rich or of the poor. God, in the Mosaic system, cautioned: "Ye shall do no unrighteousness in judgment: thou shalt not respect the person of the poor, nor honour the person of the mighty: but in righteousness shalt thou judge thy neighbour" (Lev. 19:15). Simon Peter learned this lesson at Joppa when God let down from heaven the sheet full of unclean animals and commanded him to eat of them. Peter concluded from that experience, ". . . Of a truth I perceive that God is no respecter of persons" (Acts 10:34).

James uses a stinging illustration to make his point:

> **For if there come unto your assembly a man with a gold ring, in goodly apparel, and there come in also a poor man in vile raiment [James 2:2].**

The word *assembly* here means synagogue. Evidently the Jewish Christians were calling the place where they met a synagogue. They had erected no buildings and frequently met in private homes, but the chances are that in many places they rented a synagogue. They met on Sunday rather than on Saturday and therefore did not conflict with the meeting of the Jews.

"A man with a gold ring" doesn't mean he wore a single ring, but that he had his fingers loaded down with gold rings, which was an evidence of wealth. "Goodly apparel" means that he had on fine clothes, bright clothes. He was ostentatious, if you please. His clothing is contrasted with that of the poor man.

Someone has said, "Some go to church to close their eyes, and others go to eye the clothes." We have made Sunday a time when we Christians put on our Sunday-go-to-meeting clothes. A great many people come to church overdressed. There is a dash and a splash and a flash about them. There is a pomp and pomposity. It's glitter and gaudy, and vulgar and vain, also.

This rich man makes his entrance into church with flags flying and a fanfare of trumpets. There is parade and pageant. It is as if he drives up in his gold Cadillac, getting out as his chauffer opens the door for him. He walks in, strutting like a peacock. He is like the rich man the

Lord Jesus spoke of in the true story of the rich man and Lazarus: "There was a certain rich man, which was clothed in purple and fine linen, and fared sumptuously every day" (Luke 16:19). He "fared sumptuously" means that life was one continual party for him.

In contrast, the poor man, whom James mentions here, comes in with tattered and torn clothing. It may be clean, but there is evidence of patches and poverty. He may even be shabby and shoddy. He may be dilapidated and deteriorated. He may have seen better days, but he doesn't have any Sunday clothes. James places these two men in contrast—each is at an extreme end of the social ladder.

In our affluent society we use other occasions as an excuse to dress up, but certainly many people use church as an occasion to do that. Easter Sunday is a good example of this. In Southern California, ladies usually don't wear hats to church, but on Easter Sunday we always have a parade of new hats in church. When I was a pastor I would sometimes look out over the congregation and say, "Well, they are as wild as ever!" and everybody knew I was talking about the hats. My wife told me the ladies didn't like my wisecracks, so I had to quit doing that. Another example is that when I began in the ministry I wanted to look like a preacher, and I think I really overdid it. I wore a Prince Albert coat and striped trousers. I had a wing collar and a black bow tie. I even wore a derby hat. You would have thought I was a barker in a circus or the maitre d' at the Waldorf Astoria in New York City. Then one day I looked down into the congregation at a couple who were people of means; in fact, they were very wealthy. I noticed how unostentatiously this man was dressed. He had on a highpriced suit, but it was very modest. And his wife was well dressed, but not over-dressed. I thought, *My, here I am up here dressed as a person ought not to be dressed who is coming in to worship God*. So the next Sunday I came to church in everyday clothes, and I have been wearing them ever since, just like the man who is sitting in the pew. My friend, there is a danger of putting an emphasis upon clothes.

And ye have respect to him that weareth the gay clothing, and say unto him, Sit thou here in a good place;

> **and say to the poor, Stand thou there, or sit here under
> my footstool [James 2:3].**

In our day this would be like putting the poor man way back where the
ushers sit or telling him to stand up in the rear. In that day there were a
few seats down front where only the prominent people were allowed to
sit. In the United States there was a day when we had paid pews in our
churches. They had a little door to them, and only the family which
paid for that pew could sit there on Sunday. You couldn't sit with
· whomever you wanted to sit. Today we have our little cliques who take
a certain section in a church, and woe to the stranger (especially if he
is not well dressed) who comes in and sits next to that crowd! I can
assure you he will get a cold shoulder.

> **Are ye not then partial in yourselves, and are become
> judges of evil thoughts? [James 2:4].**

After James has put these two men in contrast, he asks, "Aren't you
actually being partial in yourselves or aren't you making distinctions
among yourselves and becoming judges with evil motives?"

> **Hearken, my beloved brethren, Hath not God chosen the
> poor of this world rich in faith, and heirs of the kingdom
> which he hath promised to them that love him? [James
> 2:5].**

"Hearken, my beloved brethren"—James is talking to believers, and he
calls them "brethren."
   A poor believer certainly is looked down upon in certain churches,
and yet he may be the richest man spiritually in that church.
   The Word of God says a great deal about the poor. God has made it
very clear from Genesis to Revelation that He has a concern and consideration for the poor. It is as true in Moscow, Russia, as it is in the cities
of New York, Washington, or Los Angeles that the poor never get a fair
deal, and they never have. As long as men are natural men who are not

born-again Christians, the poor will never get a fair deal in this world. Their only hope is in Jesus Christ.

Listen to the Word of God: "But he saveth the poor from the sword, from their mouth, and from the hand of the mighty" (Job 5:15). And in Job 36:15 we read, "He delivereth the poor in his affliction, and openeth their ears in oppression." Psalm 9:18 says, "For the needy shall not alway be forgotten: the expectation of the poor shall not perish for ever." Again in Psalms we read, "Thy congregation hath dwelt therein: thou, O God, hast prepared of thy goodness for the poor" (Ps. 68:10). "For the LORD heareth the poor . . ." says Psalm 69:33. "For he shall deliver the needy when he crieth; the poor also, and him that hath no helper. He shall spare the poor and needy, and shall save the souls of the needy" (Ps. 72:12–13). Then in Psalm 102:17 we read, "He will regard the prayer of the destitute, and not despise their prayer." There is Scripture after Scripture that speaks of the poor and of God's concern for them. In marvelous Psalm 45 we read of the One who is coming who will reign on this earth in righteousness, and in Isaiah 11 we read, "But with righteousness shall he judge the poor . . ." (Isa. 11:4).

God has a great deal to say about the mistreatment of the poor on this earth by the rich and by those who are in power. Someday they will have to answer to Him for it. But the poor can be rich in spiritual things, and that is the important thing for the poor man to see.

But ye have despised the poor. Do not rich men oppress you, and draw you before the judgment seats? [James 2:6].

Whether it is at the hands of a rich corporation or of a rich labor union, the powerful are not giving the poor an honest deal. Every year the politicians come out to us when they are running for office and say that they are going to work for and help all of us poor people. It does not make any difference what political party is in power, they wind up exploiting us. If I sound rather cynical, my friend, it is because I was born a poor boy and I have not gotten very far from that even to this day.

From that viewpoint I am cynical because I have seen the way the poor are treated on this earth. Their only hope is in Jesus Christ. They have been despised by the world. The rich and powerful want their vote, but that ends their interest in them.

> **Do not they blaspheme that worthy name by the which ye are called? [James 2:7].**

Worthy is better translated as "honorable." My friend, when you mistreat the poor, you are blaspheming the name of Christ.

> **If ye fulfil the royal law according to the scripture, Thou shalt love thy neighbour as thyself, ye do well [James 2:8].**

If you want to please God, to obey Him, and to discharge your responsibility, James makes it very clear what you are to do: "Thou shalt love thy neighbour as thyself." That is the summation of the whole manward aspect of the Mosaic Law.

> **But if ye have respect to persons, ye commit sin, and are convinced of the law as transgressors [James 2:9].**

The Law condemns discriminating between the rich and poor. Someone will say, "Well, I didn't commit murder, and I haven't committed adultery." You haven't? Listen to what James says—

> **For whosoever shall keep the whole law, and yet offend in one point, he is guilty of all [James 2:10].**

James is not saying that if you break one commandment, you have broken them all. He is saying you are guilty of breaking the commandments no matter which one it is that you broke. A man may be in prison as a murderer, look across the aisle and say to another fellow, "I'm not a rapist. I never broke *that* law"—yes, but he is behind bars; he is a murderer. It is ironic when a prisoner actually murders another prisoner because he considers *his* crime a terrible thing! But, my friend, you do not have to go to the penitentiary to find that attitude; you will find people outside of prison who are looking down upon others in the same way.

We all stand before God as lawbreakers.

> **For he that said, Do not commit adultery, said also, Do not kill. Now if thou commit no adultery, yet if thou kill, thou art become a transgressor of the law [James 2:11].**

To break one law makes a lawbreaker.

> **So speak ye, and so do, as they that shall be judged by the law of liberty [James 2:12].**

The "law of liberty" is the law of Christ. The Lord Jesus said, "If ye love me, keep my commandments" (John 14:15). What is His commandment? "This is my commandment, That ye love one another, as I have loved you" (John 15:12).

> **For he shall have judgment without mercy, that hath shewed no mercy; and mercy rejoiceth against judgment [James 2:13].**

Many years ago in New York City there lived a wealthy couple by the name of Mr. and Mrs. Whitemore. They were entertaining guests one night and, in order to do something different, they went down to the Bowery to the mission of Jerry McAuley. These people went in and sat down in the back to take in the service that night. This wealthy couple belonged to a very fashionable church, but they had no more heard the Gospel than a person living in the darkest heathenism in the world. As they heard Jerry McAuley preach, their hearts were touched, and they saw themselves as sinners. They went forward, and that night the mink knelt with the rags as they accepted Christ. Mr. and Mrs. Whitemore became workers in that area, and she established a home for wayward girls. She became known as the Rose of Mulberry Bend and was instrumental in beginning the movement for a ministry to such troubled girls.

How we need to recognize today that it is *sinful* to think that we are better than someone else and to look down upon others. It does not matter who the man is; before God that man is on the same plane as you are. We are sinners and need to come as that rich couple came—we need to come to the Cross and accept Christ as our Savior.

Another story is told that took place in London when a great preacher, a very fine young man, by the name of Caesar Milan was invited one evening to a very large and prominent home where a choice musical was to be presented. On the program was a young lady who thrilled the audience with her singing and playing. When she finished, this young preacher threaded his way through the crowd which was gathered around her. When he finally came to her and had her attention, he said, "Young lady, when you were singing, I sat there and thought how tremendously the cause of Christ would be benefited if you would dedicate yourself and your talents to the Lord. But," he added, "you are just as much a sinner as the worst drunkard in the street, or any harlot on Scarlet Street. But I am glad to tell you that the blood of Jesus Christ, God's Son, will cleanse you from all sin if you will come to Him." In a very haughty manner, she turned her head aside and said to him, "You are very insulting, sir." And she started to walk away. He said, "Lady, I did not mean any offense, but I pray that the Spirit of God will convict you."

Well, they all went home, and that night this young woman could not sleep. At two o'clock in the morning she knelt at the side of her bed and took Christ as her Savior. And then she, Charlotte Elliott, sat down and, while sitting there, wrote the words of a favorite hymn, "Just As I Am":

> Just as I am, without one plea,
> But that Thy blood was shed for me,
> And that Thou bidd'st me come to Thee,
> > O Lamb of God, I come!
>
> Just as I am, and waiting not
> To rid my soul of one dark blot,

> To Thee whose blood can cleanse each spot,
> > O Lamb of God, I come!

And then the final stanza:

> Just as I am—Thou wilt receive,
> Wilt welcome, pardon, cleanse, relieve;
> Because Thy promise I believe,
> > O Lamb of God, I come!

My friend, may I say to you, that this is the basis on which all of us must come to Christ.

GOD TESTS FAITH BY GOOD WORKS

In verses 14–26 James shows that God tests faith by good works. There are those who say that we have in this section a contradiction to the writings of Paul, because Paul made it abundantly clear that faith *alone* could save you. We have his clear statement in Galatians 2:16— "Knowing that a man is *not* justified by the works of the law, but by the *faith* of Jesus Christ, even we have believed in Jesus Christ, that we might be justified by the faith of Christ, and not by the works of the law: for by the works of the law shall no flesh be justified" (italics mine).

I have divided this section up as follows: (1) The interpretation of faith (v. 14); (2) the identification of faith (vv. 15–20); and (3) the illustration of faith (vv. 21–26).

First we have the *interpretation of faith*. When we understand the definition of faith as it is used by Paul and James in the context of their writings, we can see that Paul and James are in perfect agreement, that they are discussing the same subject from different viewpoints.

Paul says that a man is not saved by the works or the deeds of the Law. In Romans 3:28 he writes, "Therefore we conclude that a man is justified by faith without the deeds of the law." In Galatians, as we have noted, Paul says that a man is justified not by works but by faith in Christ Jesus. How then are we going to reconcile Paul and James? As someone has said, "Paul and James do not stand face to face, fighting against each other, but they stand back to back, fighting opposite foes." In that day there were those who were saying that you had to perform the works of the Law (the Mosaic Law), that you had to come by the Law, in order to be saved. Paul answered that by saying that the works of the Law will not save you and that only faith in Christ can save you. Both Paul and James, therefore, are defending the citadel of *faith*. To see that, we need to understand the use of their terminology. Paul says that *saving faith*—a faith which is genuine and real—will transform a person's life. Paul said of himself, "But what things were gain to me those I counted loss for Christ" (Phil. 3:7). A real revolution took place in his life when he came to Christ. In 1 Corinthians 15:1–2 Paul wrote, "Moreover, brethren, I declare unto you the gospel which I preached unto you, which also ye have received, and wherein ye stand; By which also ye are *saved*, if ye keep in memory what I preached unto you, unless ye have believed in vain;" that is, unless it was just an empty faith (italics mine). Now let us look at what James has to say—

> **What doth it profit, my brethren, though a man say he hath faith, and have not works? can faith save him? [James 2:14].**

James is not talking about the works of the Law. He simply says that the faith which saves you *will* produce works, works of faith. The faith that James is talking about here is *professing faith*, that which is phony and counterfeit. Paul refers to the same idea when he says in 1 Corinthians 15:2, " . . . unless ye have believed in vain." Paul also wrote, "Examine yourselves, whether ye be in the faith . . ." (2 Cor. 13:5).

One of the greatest dangers for us preachers of the Gospel is that we like to see people converted, and we are willing to accept a brazen and flippant yes from some individual who says, "Yes, I'll trust Jesus." However, it might be just an impertinent, impudent, and insolent nod of the head; it is so easy today to be as phony as a three-dollar bill.

The story is told that the Devil had a meeting with his demons to decide how to persuade men that God was nonexistent. Since they themselves believed in His existence, they wondered just how to do it.

One demon suggested that they tell people Jesus Christ never really existed and that men should not believe such fiction. Another demon suggested that they persuade men that death ends all and there is no need to worry about life after death. Finally, the most intelligent demon suggested that they tell everyone that there is a God, that there is Jesus Christ, and that believing in Him saves, but all you have to do is profess faith in Christ and then go on living in sin as you used to. They decided to use this tactic, and it is the tactic the Devil uses even today.

Paul and James are in perfect harmony in their teaching. When Paul speaks of works, it is *works of the Law*. He says in Romans 3:20, "Therefore by the deeds of the law there shall no flesh be justified in his sight: for by the law is the knowledge of sin." He is saying in effect, "Yes, the Law is a mirror—it reveals you are a sinner—but it cannot save you; the works of the Law cannot save you at all." James also says that you have to have something more than just the works of the Law. He wrote, "For whosoever shall keep the whole law and yet offend in one point, he is guilty of all" (v. 10). As someone has put it, "Man cannot be saved by perfect obedience, for he cannot render it. He cannot be saved by imperfect obedience because God will not accept it." The only solution to this dilemma is the redemption that is in Christ Jesus, and both James and Paul emphasize that.

In Galatians 2:16 Paul made it clear that men are not saved by the Law, but later in that epistle he wrote, "And let us not be weary in well-doing . . ." (Gal. 6:9). There is a lot of *doing* that goes with *believing*. "Let him that is taught in the word communicate unto him that teacheth in all good things. Be not deceived; God is not mocked: for whatsoever a man soweth, that shall he also reap" (Gal. 6:6–7). In this section of his epistle when James speaks of works, he is speaking of the *works of faith*. Paul also wrote about works of faith: "For in Jesus Christ neither circumcision availeth any thing, nor uncircumcision; but faith which worketh by love" (Gal. 5:6). Both of these men taught that faith must be a working faith. As John Calvin put it, "Faith alone saves, but the faith that saves is not alone."

Saving faith, therefore, is alive; professing faith is dead. We have a lot of so-called professing Christians today who are members of churches. They are nothing in the world but zombies. They are walking around as if they are alive, but they are dead.

A girl once asked her Sunday School teacher, "How can I be a Christian and still have my own way?" The teacher gave to her Romans 8:5 which says, "For they that are after the flesh do mind the things of the flesh; but they that are after the Spirit the things of the Spirit." If you are a child of God, you cannot have your own way. You are going to do His way. "Because the carnal mind is enmity against God: for it is not subject to the law of God, neither indeed can be. . . . But ye are not in the flesh, but in the Spirit, if so be that the Spirit of God dwell in you . . ." (Romans 8:7, 9). Paul says that now that you are indwelt by the Spirit of God, you can produce the fruit of the Spirit in your life; if you don't, there is something radically wrong. A Christian doesn't do as he pleases; he does as Christ pleases.

During the depression there lived in Pittsburgh a tycoon who was having all kinds of problems in his life. He went to his pastor and, after talking over his problems, he said, "I love my Savior. I love my family. I love my church. I love my business. But there are times I feel like walking out on all four of them." The pastor looked him straight in the eye and said, "Well, why don't you?" The man replied, "The reason I don't is that I am a Christian." May I say to you, saving faith which makes one a Christian will lead to good works. However, we are so anxious to get church members that we accept them on the slightest profession. As a result, many churches are filled with professing Christians who are really unbelievers.

When we understand how Paul and James use the words *faith* and *works*, we can see that they are in total agreement in their teaching.

Now James deals with the *identification of faith*. Saving faith can be recognized and identified by certain spiritual fingerprints. There is a verification of genuine faith. James gives us this practical illustration—

> **If a brother or sister be naked, and destitute of daily food,**
>
> **And one of you say onto them, Depart in peace, be ye warmed and filled; notwithstanding ye give them not**

those things which are needful to the body; what doth it profit? [James 2:15–16].

Pious clichés and Christian verbiage are not the evidence of saving faith. There must be a vocation to go along with the vocabulary. You can be very pious and say to an individual, "Brother, I will pray for you, and I know the Lord will provide." My friend, the Lord put you there as a child of God to do the providing. I get a little weary sometimes when wealthy Christian laymen pat me on the back and say, "Dr. McGee, you are doing a fine thing. You are doing the right thing in giving out the Word of God," but they do not have a part in supporting this ministry financially. I have a hard time believing they are sincere. You may piously say to someone, "Oh, brother, I'm for you." Are you for him? Are you back of him? My friend, a living faith *produces* something—you can *identify* it.

The Lord Jesus said, "By this shall all men know that ye are my disciples, if ye have love one to another" (John 13:35). Then in Romans 13:8, Paul says, "Owe no man any thing, but to love one another: for he that loveth another hath fulfilled the law." The point is that you cannot say you are a child of God and live like a lawless individual. I do not mean that whenever a bum asks you for twenty-five cents in order to buy wine you should give it to him. And I do not think that you should believe every individual who professes to be a Christian. We need to test them out to see whether they are or not. My heart is warmed when I think of a certain man I know who is rendering financial assistance to someone in need and of a lady of means who is supporting a missionary abroad and telling no one about it. May I say to you, you are telling by your life whether your faith is genuine or not.

Even so faith, if it hath not works, is dead, being alone.

Yea, a man may say, Thou hast faith, and I have works: shew me thy faith without thy works, and I will shew thee my faith by my works [James 2:17–18].

"Faith, if it hath not works, is dead." The faith is dead? Why? Because living faith, saving faith, produces works. You have to draw that conclusion from James' illustration. He is talking about the fruit of faith. Paul talks about the root of faith. Those are the separate emphases of each man, but both Paul and James say that faith alone saves. Paul also says that faith is going to produce fruit—"But the fruit of the Spirit is love, joy, peace . . ." (Gal. 5:22). The Lord Jesus said, "I am the vine, ye are the branches: He that abideth in me, and I in him, the same bringeth forth much fruit . . ." (John 15:5).

A minister once talked to a man who professed conversion, and he asked, "Have you united with the church?" "No, I haven't," the man replied. "The dying thief never united with the church, and he went to heaven." The minister asked, "Have you ever sat at the Lord's table?" "No, the dying thief never did, and he was accepted" was the answer. The minister asked, "Have you been baptized?" "No," he said, "the dying thief was never baptized, and he went to heaven." "Have you given to missions?" "No, the dying thief did not give to missions, and he was not judged for it" was the reply. Then this disgusted minister said to the man, "Well, my friend, the difference between you two seems to be that he was a dying thief and you are a living thief."

My friend, we often sing, "O for a thousand tongues to sing my great Redeemer's praise," but we do not even use the one tongue we have. And we sing, "Were the whole realm of nature mine, that were a present far too small," and then we give nothing at all to Him. James says it is faith that saves, but saving faith produces something.

> **Thou believest that there is one God; thou doest well: the devils also believe, and tremble [James 2:19].**

Lip service is not the evidence of saving faith—even the demons believe.

> **But wilt thou know, O vain man, that faith without works is dead? [James 2:20].**

Faith without the fruit of faith is empty and futile as far as the world is concerned.

Now James will give us the *illustration of faith*—in fact, there will be two illustrations.

> **Was not Abraham our father justified by works, when he had offered Isaac his son upon the altar?**
>
> **Seest thou how faith wrought with his works, and by works was faith made perfect?**
>
> **And the scripture was fulfilled which saith, Abraham believed God, and it was imputed unto him for righteousness: and he was called the Friend of God.**
>
> **Ye see then how that by works a man is justified, and not by faith only [James 2:21-24].**

Paul said that Abraham was justified by *faith* (see Rom. 4:3), and Genesis tells us that he was justified by *faith* (see Gen. 15:6; 22:1–14). Was Abraham justified when he offered his son Isaac? The question is: *Did he offer his son Isaac?* And the answer is: No, he didn't. Then what was Abraham's work of faith? How did works save him? His faith caused him to lift that knife to do a thing which he did not believe God would ever ask him to do. But since God had asked him, he was willing to do it. He believed that God would raise Isaac from the dead. Abraham never actually offered Isaac, because God provided a substitute, but he would have done it if God had not stopped him.

This is a choice illustration of the fact that you demonstrate your faith by your actions. The action of this man was that *he believed God*.

James uses a second illustration—

> **Likewise also was not Rahab the harlot justified by works, when she had received the messengers, and had sent them out another way? [James 2:25].**

How was Rahab justified by works? She received the Israelite spies, concealed them from her own people, then told them how to escape without being detected (see Josh. 2). That woman living there in the city of Jericho jeopardized her life by turning her back on her old life and on her own people. What was gain to her became loss. She did not say to the Israelite spies, "I'll just stand on the sidelines when you enter the city and sing, 'Praise God from whom all blessings flow.'" She did not just say, "Jesus saves and keeps and satisfies." She did not say, "Hallelujah! Praise the Lord!" She said to them, "I'm going to *do* something. I will hide you because I believe God is going to give the people of Israel this land. We have been hearing about you for forty years, and I believe God." My friend, she believed God, and she became involved. She was justified before God by her faith: "By faith the harlot Rahab perished not with them that believed not, when she had received the spies with peace" (Heb. 11:31). However, before her own people and before the Israelites, she was justified by works.

Many years ago I went to a nursery and bought a bare root which was labeled "Santa Rosa plum." It wasn't even as big as a broom handle, and it looked no more alive than a broom handle. I was told to put it in the ground in a certain way, and I did that. I watched it, and the next spring it began to shoot out leaves. In three years there were blossoms on it, and then there was fruit. Do you know what kind of fruit was on that tree? Plums. The root of that tree was a plum root.

Faith is the root, and the root produces the kind of fruit that the root itself is. If you have a living faith, there is going to be fruit in your life. Paul says, "Examine yourselves, whether ye be in the faith; prove your own selves . . ." (2 Cor. 13:5).

And James continues—

For as the body without the spirit is dead, so faith without works is dead also [James 2:26].

Faith without works is like a dead body in a morgue. James said that; Paul said that, and Vernon McGee believes both of them because they are giving us God's Word for it.

CHAPTER 3

THEME: *God tests faith by the tongue*

GOD TESTS FAITH BY THE TONGUE

I have written a booklet on the third chapter of James, and it has a sensational title; but my sensationalism is no greater than that of the Bible, for my title is a Bible title: *Hell on Fire.* We will see that that is the expression James uses here in talking about the tongue.

We have heard a great deal in recent years about freedom of speech and freedom of the press, and it has become sort of a sacred cow. However, freedom of the press in our day means that they can brainwash you according to the liberal viewpoint, and freedom of speech means that you can use vile language. I would like for someone to grant us freedom of hearing. I have only one mouth, but I have two ears, and I think my ears ought to be protected as well as my mouth. We need freedom of hearing today as well as freedom of speech.

This chapter deals with "Freedom of Speech in God's University," which is another way I have labeled this particular chapter. I also like the title, "God Bugs Your Conversation." There is no question that God has the right to bug, or to listen in on, our conversations. He has had that right for a long time, and He has heard everything that you and I have said. It is estimated that the average person says about thirty thousand words every day. (I know two or three people who exceed that number!) That is enough to make a good-sized book. In a lifetime, you or I could fill a library with the words we have said. God has that recorded, by the way, because He bugs your conversation.

I suppose that the present-day movement for freedom of speech began at the Berkeley campus of the University of California some years ago. It was given coverage by the news media out of all proportion to its importance; that news coverage itself was another attempt at brainwashing. A great many taxpayers and prominent citizens were concerned that this great university, which is supported by their tax money, could be shut down and made a ridiculous spectacle by a few radicals, while the majority of the students were intimidated and their good intentions of getting an education were reflected upon.

Now the problem of freedom of speech is not only out yonder in the university and in the news media, but it is in the church also. The problem in the church is the problem of gossip. Each one of us who is a Christian needs to be concerned about our freedom of speech.

Just as I do with the Book of Proverbs, I liken the Epistle of James to a course in God's university. James is the dean of God's university as we consider this controversial subject, and he has quite a bit to say concerning the use and abuse of the tongue. We have seen in this epistle that God tests faith in many different ways. Here God tests our faith by our tongue. We want to reach up on the shelf of the laboratory of life and take down an acid to test our faith. Actually, this acid is more potent than hydrochloric or sulfuric or any other acid. The label on the bottle is "Tongue."

However, we are not talking about the chemistry of the tongue but about the theology of the tongue. James has already indicated that he was going to come to this subject. He said back in chapter 1, verse 26, "If any man among you seem to be religious, and bridleth not his tongue, but deceiveth his own heart, this man's religion is vain." He also said, "let every man be swift to hear, slow to speak" (James 1:19). You have two ears, and God gave them to you so that you can hear twice as much as you can say.

The tongue is the most dangerous weapon in the world. It is more deadly than the atom bomb, but no careful inspection is made of it. Some wag made the statement that it was a miracle in Balaam's day for an ass to speak, but today it is a miracle when he keeps quiet. Someone else pointed out that it takes a baby two years to learn to talk and fifty years to learn to keep his mouth shut.

The story is told of a man who had been fishing out on a pier for several hours and had not caught anything. As two women walked out on the pier, he finally pulled in a fish. It wasn't a very large fish, and one of these two women took it upon herself to rebuke this man: "Aren't you ashamed of yourself for so cruelly catching this poor little fish?" And the man, without even looking up, because he was a little discouraged anyway, said, "Maybe you are right, lady, but if the fish had kept his mouth shut he wouldn't have been caught."

Another has expressed it this way:

> If your lips would keep from slips,
> Five things to observe with care:
> To whom you speak, of whom you speak,
> And how, and when, and where.
> —Author unknown

The importance of the tongue has been expressed in many different ways, and practically every nation has had something to say about it. I read this in Spurgeon's "Salt Cellars" years ago:

> "The boneless tongue so small and weak,
> Can crush and kill," declared the Greek.
> "The tongue destroys a greater hoard,"
> The Turk asserts, "than does the sword."

> A Persian proverb wisely saith,
> "A lengthy tongue—an early death";
> Or sometimes takes this form instead,
> "Don't let your tongue cut off your head."

> "The tongue can speak a word whose speed,"
> The Chinese say, "outstrips the steed";
> While Arab sages this impart,
> "The tongue's great storehouse is the heart."

> From Hebrew wit this maxim sprung,
> "Though feet should slip, ne'er let the tongue."
> The sacred writer crowns the whole,
> "Who keeps his tongue doth keep his soul!"

All of these sayings are very wise. I believe fervently that the most dangerous thing in the world is the tongue. I think the church is more harmed by the termites within than by the woodpeckers on the outside. Someone has put it like this: "Thou art master of the unspoken word, but the spoken word is master of you." In other words, my friend, once you have said it, it is beyond your control.

All of that is preliminary. Let us look now at what James has to say concerning the tongue—

My brethren, be not many masters, knowing that we shall receive the greater condemnation [James 3:1].

Masters means "teachers." James is saying that a teacher has a greater responsibility, and the reason for that is the grave danger of teaching the wrong thing. I am absolutely amazed and overwhelmed at the way so many Christian folk fall for all kinds of teaching, particularly that which has to do with prophecy. All a teacher needs today is a glib tongue. People are accepting all kinds of methods and cults and "isms"; yet many of these teachers, as far as the total Word of God is concerned, are absolutely ignorant. I rejoice in home Bible classes, and I think they have filled a real vacuum that existed, but I find that some of the leaders are teaching all kinds of vagaries, giving the wrong interpretation of Scripture. They need to know more of the Word of God than they do.

The ease with which people fall for their teachings has ministered to a great deal of conceit and pride on the part of many teachers. One young fellow that I had the privilege of leading to Christ has gone off on a tangent in his teaching. I tried to get him to study the Word, but he did not. He has now started a class, and he is very glib of tongue. Someone in his class went to him and said, "Do you know that what you have taught is contrary to most Bible teachers and especially to the man who led you to the Lord?" The young man replied, "Oh, Dr. McGee? Well, maybe he needs to correct *his* theology." Well, frankly, maybe I do. I am amazed the more I study the Word of God. The thing that discourages me is that it reveals my ignorance, not my knowledge. I realize I have a long way to go, but the young man who made that statement has even farther to go. However, he does not recognize his own ignorance.

I am reminded of what a preacher said of another young man who had just started out in the ministry. When someone pointed out his prideful attitude, the preacher said of the young man, "Yes, he thinks he is the fourth person of the Trinity." It is so easy for a preacher or teacher to become proud.

The tongue is very dangerous. James is saying here, "My brethren, be not many teachers." Don't think that the minute you become a child of God you can start a Bible class and teach the Book of Revelation.

"Knowing that we shall receive the greater condemnation." Frankly, it is frightening to realize that God will judge us for the way in which we teach His Word, and we will be under His condemnation if our teaching is wrong. My friend, the more opportunity you have to give out the Word of God, the greater is your responsibility to God Himself.

> **For in many things we offend all. If any man offend not in word, the same is a perfect man, and able also to bridle the whole body [James 3:2].**

"For in many things we offend all" means that in many ways we all stumble. All of us do—there is no exception to that.

"If any man offend not in word the same is a perfect man." The word *perfect* means he is a full-grown Christian as he should be—just as a baby grows up, becomes a little child and matures to full adulthood.

James says the perfect man is "able also to bridle the whole body." In other words, if he can control his speech, he can control his entire body, in fact, his whole life. The tongue lifts man from the animal world. It keeps him from being a gibbering ape or an aping parrot. Man is not an inarticulate animal or a mockingbird. Man can put thought into words; he can express himself; he can be understood; he can communicate on the highest level. The tongue is a badge which you and I wear—it identifies us. It is the greatest index to life. It is the table of contents of our lives.

Our tongues give us away; they tell who we are. Quite a few years ago I was rushing with my wife and little girl from a conference at Salt Lake City to a conference in the San Francisco Bay area. As we came

over the High Sierras and Donner Pass, we stopped at a little town—I
don't even know the name of it—and pulled into a filling station. I
stepped out of the car and said to the young man there, "Fill 'er up!"
That's all I said, but as I was looking out at those mountains and the
lovely scenery, I became conscious that he was eyeing me. Finally, I
turned to him and smiled. He said to me, "Are you Dr. McGee?" I said,
"I sure am. Do I know you?" He said, "No." I said, "Do you know me?"
He said, "No. I've never seen you before, but up here, especially during the wintertime when we are all snowed in, we listen to you every
Sunday night on the radio. We've been doing it for years. I'd know
your voice anywhere." I've had that same experience a number of
times. You see, my tongue gives me away.

Remember the maid who said to Simon Peter, " . . . thy speech
betrayeth thee" (Matt. 26:73)—he could not deny that he was from Gal-
ilee. Your speech tells who you are; your tongue gives you away. It tells
where you came from. It tells whether you are ignorant or educated,
cultured or crude, whether you are clean or unclean, whether you are
vulgar or refined, whether you are a believer or a blasphemer, whether
you are a Christian or a non-Christian, whether you are guilty or not
guilty. My friend, I am of the opinion that if you had a tape-recorded
message of everything you have said this past month, you would not
want the world to hear it.

Now let's put the acid down on your tongue and mine. James will
first deal with the unbridled and unrestrained tongue—

> **Behold, we put bits in the horses' mouths, that they may
> obey us; and we turn about their whole body [James
> 3:3].**

The illustration James uses here is the horse. It was David who said, "I
said, I will take heed to my ways, that I sin not with my tongue: I will
keep my mouth with a bridle, while the wicked is before me" (Ps.
39:1). In other words, David said that because he wanted to give the
right kind of testimony, he would put a bridle on his mouth. My
friend, there are a lot of Christians today who ought to have a bridle put
on their mouths.

The bridle bits are not impressive in size, but they can hold a high-spirited horse in check and keep him from running away. If you are old enough, you may have recollections of the horse-and-buggy days. I can recall seeing a horse run away, turn over a buggy, and bring death and destruction to a family. In the same way, the tongue can run away. Someone said of another individual, "His mind starts his tongue to wagging, and then goes off and leaves it." We should not go through life like that—there needs to be a bridle for the tongue.

Now James is going to use a different illustration—

Behold also the ships, which though they be so great, and are driven of fierce winds, yet are they turned about with a very small helm, whithersoever the governor listeth [James 3:4].

Large ships can be controlled by a little rudder which few people even see. A fierce storm may drive a ship, but a little rudder can control it. The tongue can also change the course of our lives. Men have been ruined by the tongue; many the fair name of a woman has been wrecked by some gossipy tongue.

James says that the tongue is more dangerous than a runaway horse or a storm at sea. I believe that liquor is eating at the vitals of our nation today, but did you know that the tongue is condemned more in Scripture than alcoholism is condemned? Liquor and alcoholism may bring our nation down, yet the tongue is even more dangerous than that. Proverbs 6:16–17 says, "These six things doth the LORD hate: yea, seven are an abomination unto him: A proud look, a lying tongue, and hands that shed innocent blood." A lying tongue is one of the seven things God hates.

The tongue can really get us into trouble—there is no question about that. Again, someone has put it in words like this:

> A careless word may kindle strife;
> A cruel word may wreck a life.
> A bitter word may hate instill;
> A brutal word may smite and kill.

> A gracious word may smooth the way;
> A joyous word may light the day.
> A timely word may lessen stress;
> A loving word may heal and bless.
>   —Author unknown

I was very impressed when I read General Montgomery's farewell words addressed to the Eighth Army in Italy following World War II. He said to them, "Command must be personal and it must be verbal; otherwise it will have no success, because it is wrapped up in the human factor." Continuing, he said this: "I often have at the back of my mind a passage from the New Testament, 'Except ye utter by the tongue words easy to be understood, how shall it be known what is spoken?'" (see 1 Cor. 14:9). That is the kind of tongue I want to have as I teach the Word of God—the tongue that both a little child and the older folk can understand. Someone asked me one time, "How in the world can the same message bring a nine-year-old child and a university professor to the Lord?" I must confess, I do not know the answer to that question. But I do believe that God blesses His Word and that it must be taught simply. We must put the cookies on the bottom shelf where the kiddies can get them. God did not say, "Feed My giraffes"; He said, "Feed My lambs" (see John 21.15).

Even so the tongue is a little member, and boasteth great things. Behold, how great a matter a little fire kindleth!

And the tongue is a fire, a world of iniquity: so is the tongue among our members, that it defileth the whole body, and setteth on fire the course of nature; and it is set on fire of hell [James 3:5–6].

This is where I got the title for my little book on this third chapter of James, *Hell on Fire.* That is what the tongue can be and is in many cases. There are those who have questioned my use of the word *hell,* arguing that it is not properly translated in this verse. The Greek word used here is *gehenna;* it is not *sheol.* It refers to the valley of Hinnom where the fire never went out. This word is used only twelve times in the New Testament; the Lord Jesus used it eleven times, and James used it once. This is a correct translation: the tongue is "set on fire of hell."

It is quite impressive that James compares the tongue to a fire. I do not know whether you have ever seen a forest fire, but each summer out here in California we have an epidemic of them. They are very devastating, and many times absolutely uncontrollable; they have to burn themselves out in many instances.

Fire has been, of course, one of the greatest friends of man and nature. Some historians say that civilization began when man discovered fire. When it is under control, it warms our bodies, it cooks our food, and it generates power to turn the wheels of industry. It is dangerous, though, when it is out of control. It is a tragedy when a house is on fire. You hear a siren in the night, and you know that a group of men is rushing to put out a fire. Even in our present civilization we are not able to control fires. The London fire of 1666 destroyed London. Mrs. O'Leary's cow kicked over a lantern in Chicago in 1871 and started that great and historic fire. And still today we see great devastations caused by fire.

The tongue is like a fire; when it is under control, it is a blessing; when it is out of control, it is devastating. It can be a cure, or it can be a curse. In Proverbs 12:18 we read, "There is that speaketh like the piercings of a sword: but the tongue of the wise is health." The tongue can be like a sword that kills, but it also can be health itself. What a picture this is of the tongue! Again in Proverbs we read, "The heart of him that hath understanding seeketh knowledge: but the mouth of fools feedeth on foolishness"(Prov. 15:14).

Let me repeat the proverb I quoted a little earlier: "Thou art master of the unspoken word, but the spoken word is master of you." If you haven't said it, you cannot be held responsible, but once you've said it, it can condemn you. I have learned through personal experience that a slip of the tongue (especially if it's made on a radio broadcast which is heard by many) can have great repercussions. You remember that Simon Peter's tongue betrayed him, and he denied that he knew his Lord. But on the Day of Pentecost, what was it that the Lord used? It was the tongue of that blundering, stumbling, bumbling fellow, Simon Peter. The tongue can be either a curse or a cure.

Brush and forest fires scorch and blacken and are a plague. Like a fire, the tongue can burn through a church, burn through a community, burn through a town, and even burn through a nation.

> **For every kind of beasts, and of birds, and of serpents, and of things in the sea, is tamed, and hath been tamed of mankind:**
>
> **But the tongue can no man tame; it is an unruly evil, full of deadly poison [James 3:7–8].**

In my younger days, when the circus was coming to town, a group of us young folk would gather at some home, have a time of fellowship and a late dinner, then go down to the railroad yards to watch the circus come in and unload. As the parade of moving it out to the circus grounds was in progress, we would go along with it and then watch the tent being put up. One time we were even invited to have breakfast with them in the cook tent. My, what a thrill that was! Clyde Beatty was then with the Ringling Brothers, Barnum and Bailey Circus, and he had charge of the wild animals. He was the one who went into the cages and put them through their paces. We were in that tent, not as paid customers, but just watching them put up everything. Clyde Beatty went to a cage in which there were some little lion cubs; I think there were three or four of them. He took them out and began to play with them. He rolled them, and they bit at him; he grabbed them and turned them over, just having a big time with them. We went over and asked him why he did that. He said this: "I would never go into a cage with a lion that I had not brought up from the time it was a cub. You cannot train an old lion. I begin with these little ones, and when they grow up into fine, fierce-looking young lions, I will take them into the cage with me. But they know me, and I know them." May I say to you, you can tame a lion; you can tame an elephant, but you cannot tame the little tongue. As someone has said, "The most untamable thing in the world has its den just behind the teeth." That's one little animal which no zoo has in captivity, no circus can make it perform, no man can tame it. Only a regenerate tongue in a redeemed body, a tongue that God has tamed, can be used for Him.

It is interesting to note that Paul said, "That if thou shalt *confess with thy mouth* the Lord Jesus, and shalt *believe in thine heart* that God hath raised him from the dead, thou shalt be saved" (Rom. 10:9, italics mine). In other words, we are to sing a duet; the tongue and the heart are to be in tune. The Lord Jesus said, " . . . for out of the abundance of the heart the mouth speaketh" (Matt. 12:34)—what is in the heart will come out. Someone has said, "What is in the well of the heart will come out through the bucket of the mouth." If it is in your heart, you are going to say it sooner or later. It is interesting that when our Lord came to that dumb man, the gospel writer is very careful to say, "He touched his mouth!" My friend, if He has touched you, He has touched your mouth also.

> **Therewith bless we God, even the Father; and therewith curse we men, which are made after the similitude of God.**
>
> **Out of the same mouth proceedeth blessing and cursing. My brethren, these things ought not so to be [James 3:9–10].**

The tongues which you and I have are capable of praising God or blaspheming God. As we have said before, the tongue is that which lifts man above the animal world. Man is not a gibbering ape or a mockingbird. Man can communicate with man, and he can communicate with God. When a man can sing like an angel on Sunday and then talk like a demon during the week—you label him as you want to—the Bible calls that man a hypocrite.

When I announced in the bank where I worked as a young man that I was going to study for the ministry, one of the vice-presidents of the bank called me into his office. He had been a good friend of mine, and he knew something of my life and how I had lived. He said to me, "Vernon, I hope you are going to be a genuine preacher and a genuine servant of God." He said, "The reason I am not a Christian today is because of an experience I had during the war." (He was referring to

World War I.) He went on to tell me how the bank had set up a branch bank at the powder plant at Old Hickory outside of Nashville, Tennessee. One of the tellers there was also a soloist in a church in downtown Nashville. One Sunday as that teller came out of church, the bank vice-president overheard one of the ladies say, "You know, that man is one of the most wonderful men in the world. He sings just like an angel!" This vice-president made no comment at the time. But that woman owned property, and she had business at the bank out at Old Hickory. She came in one day and was talking to him when suddenly they heard the vilest language imaginable. It came from the teller who had attempted to balance and he hadn't balanced. (I was a teller for several years, and I know that this is one of the most discouraging things that can happen.) Well, when this man didn't balance, he began to explode with blasphemies, and the lady said, "Who in the world is that?" The bank vice-president said, "That's your soloist who sings like an angel on Sunday!" A man can bless God with his mouth, and he can blaspheme God. You can do both with the mouth you have. The Lord Jesus said that what is in the heart will come up through the mouth; you can be sure your tongue is going to say it.

> **Doth a fountain send forth at the same place sweet water and bitter?**

> **Can the fig tree, my brethren, bear olive berries? either a vine, figs? so can no fountain both yield salt water and fresh [James 3:11–12].**

In other words, a man can be a two-faced, double-minded, and forked-tongued individual—he can say both good and bad. But no fountain down here on this earth is going to give forth both sweet and bitter water, nor will a tree bear both figs and olives.

Now the tongue reveals genuine faith, because it is with the mouth that confession is made of that which is in the heart—

> **Who is a wise man and endued with knowledge among you? let him shew out of a good conversation his works with meekness of wisdom [James 3:13].**

The tongue can reveal genuine faith. It can give a testimony for God. It can speak wisdom.

But if ye have bitter envying and strife in your hearts, glory not, and lie not against the truth [James 3:14].

Strife and bitterness are certainly not the fruits of faith, but the tongue can stir up that kind of thing. James is making a contrast between the tongue of the foolish believer and the tongue of the wise believer. In fact, an uncontrolled tongue raises the question in the minds of others whether a man is a child of God or not. You cannot make me believe that a genuine believer can curse six days a week and then sing in a choir on Sunday. He cannot tell dirty jokes and then teach a Sunday School class, telling about the love of Jesus. That tongue which you have can do either one, but if it does both, it is that which stirs up strife. We are told here, "Lie not against the truth." A lying tongue is one that denies the Lord during the week by its conversation.

This wisdom descendeth not from above, but is earthly, sensual, devilish [James 3:15].

James makes it very clear that strife and envying do not originate with God. They do not come from Him at all—it is "earthly, sensual, devilish."

Knowledge is proud that she has learned so much; Wisdom is humble that she knows no more.

—Author unknown

For where envying and strife is, there is confusion and every evil work [James 3:16].

An uncontrolled tongue produces envying and strife which lead to "confusion and every evil work." Scripture makes it very clear that God is not the author of confusion. The confusion we find in the world today is a confusion brought about by the work of the Devil using that little thing, the tongue, which causes so much trouble. This verse will tie in very closely with what James has to say in the next chapter where he will define what worldliness really is.

> **But the wisdom that is from above is first pure, then peaceable, gentle, and easy to be entreated, full of mercy and good fruits, without partiality, and without hypocrisy [James 3:17].**

"But the wisdom that is from above is first pure"—that is, it's not mingled or mixed; it's undiluted; it's the original. It is that wisdom which comes down from God, and James clearly identifies it: it is "then peaceable, gentle, and easy to be entreated, full of mercy and good fruits, without partiality, and without hypocrisy."

Dr. Samuel Zwemer mentions the fact that false teaching always produces strife and envy and trouble. He says, "You cannot explain the wickedness of the world as merely human. It is human plus something, and that is why non-Christian religions are successful. They are supernatural, but from beneath." Anything that causes divisions and strife—it matters not which church it is in—is not of the Lord, you may be sure of that. You may boast of your fundamentalism, but if you are causing strife, you are sailing under false colors.

> **And the fruit of righteousness is sown in peace of them that make peace [James 3:18].**

These are the fruits of faith. There must be righteousness before there can be peace. I wish this idea would reach the United Nations. I wish it would reach Washington, D.C., and Moscow and Peking and all the other capitals of the world. You cannot have peace without righteousness. There is a day coming, the psalmist says, when peace and righteousness will have kissed each other (see Ps. 85:10). Today they don't even know each other; they wouldn't even recognize each other.

Chapter 3 concludes the first major division of the Epistle of James in which James has dealt with the verification of genuine faith. There is a difference in faith: you can believe the wrong thing, or you can just nod your head and call that faith, but *saving faith* is that which produces good works.

In these three chapters James has shown various ways in which God tests our faith to prove that it is genuine. First of all, God tests faith by trials. Dr. Richard H. Seume is an outstanding Bible teacher who has suffered with kidney trouble for a number of years. I would like to share with you something which he said (as quoted by Dr. Lehman Strauss in his book, *James Your Brother*), because I know that it comes from a preacher who is not giving us his theory or his ideas but who knows what it means to suffer. Dr. Seume wrote:

> Life on earth would not be worth much if every source of irritation were removed. Yet most of us rebel against the things that irritate us, and count as heavy loss what ought to be rich gain. We are told that the oyster is wiser; that when an irritating object, like a bit of sand, gets under the mantle of his shell, he simply covers it with the most precious part of his being and makes of it a pearl. The irritation that it was causing is stopped by encrusting it with the pearly formation. A true pearl is therefore simply a VICTORY over irritation. Every irritation that gets into our lives today is an opportunity for pearl culture. The more irritations the devil flings at us, the more pearls we may have. We need only to welcome them and cover them completely with love, that most precious part of us, and the irritation will be smothered out as the pearl comes into being. What a store of pearls we may have, if we will!

We saw, therefore, that (1) God tests faith by trials; (2) God does not test faith with evil; (3) God tests faith by the Word; (4) God tests faith by attitude and action in respect of persons; (5) God tests faith by good works; and (6) God tests faith by the tongue. James has made it very clear that genuine faith will be evident in the life of the believer.

CHAPTER 4

THEME: Vacuity and vapidness of worldliness

VACUITY AND VAPIDNESS OF WORLDLINESS

James will deal with several very important questions in this chapter: What is worldliness? How does a Christian fight the Devil? What is your life? All of these will anchor back into the subject of worldliness.

James will first answer the question: What is worldliness? I believe the average Christian in our so-called fundamental churches would give one of several answers. Some would say that worldliness is a matter of the kind of amusements you attend or indulge in: What kind of movies do you go to? Do you dance? And, do you drink? That is what they would call worldliness. May I say to you, James would not agree with them.

Others would say that it is the kind of crowd you run with, the gang you hang around with. After all, birds of a feather flock together, and if you are with a worldly crowd that engages in these things, then you are worldly. I am sorry to have to tell you, if you gave that answer in James' college, you would fail; you wouldn't pass the course.

Still others would say that worldliness is a matter of the conversation you engage in. You must learn to say "Praise the Lord" and "Hallelujah" at the right times. Worldliness is when you engage in worldly conversation. Again, that is not the answer; you have failed the course.

Someone else will answer that worldliness is the way that you dress. I have news for you: you have not passed the course.

Others may say it is a person who engages in business and the making of money to the exclusion of all else and who neglects the church; that person, they say, is a worldly individual. You still have not passed the course in James' college.

Yet another may answer that it is the person who does not go to church, but spends time on the golf course, fishing, boating, or watching his favorite team play baseball.

My friend, I do not approve of any of the things which I have mentioned here, but they just don't happen to be worldliness. Most of those sins are sins of the flesh—not of the world. If you put down any one of those as your answer to James' question, you have flunked the exam; you've failed the subject, and you've busted the course. None of those answers is correct. They may be symptoms of the disease, but nobody ever died of symptoms—they die of the disease. These are simply evidences of the real problem, which is deeper.

A brother of Henry Ward Beecher, a pastor in upper New York state, had a clock in his church that never would keep accurate time. So this man put a sign under that clock which read: "Don't blame the hands. The trouble lies deeper." This is what we need to recognize in ourselves. What we call worldliness is just the hands of the clock; the real trouble lies deeper.

William Thackeray, who was a Christian, dealt with this subject in his novel, *Vanity Fair*, in a way that probably no one else has dealt with it. His novel is about the world, and he wrote it on the background of the wars of Napoleon. He presents characters who are all filled with weaknesses and littleness, pettiness and jealousy, envy, discord and strife—all of that is there. Someone once asked Thackeray, "Why don't you have some wonderful heroes in your novels? You always present *little* people." Thackeray replied, "I hold a mirror up to nature, and I do not find heroes among mankind. They are filled with littleness and pettiness and strife and sin." When you get to the end of *Vanity Fair*, Thackeray does a masterly thing. He says, "Come, children, let us shut up the box and the puppets, for our play is played out." That is man. As Shakespeare said, he "struts and frets his hour upon the stage." Man is filled with worldliness.

Dr. Griffith Thomas pinned it down a little closer when a person who was very much distressed came to him one day and asked, "Don't you think that the world is becoming Christian today?" Dr. Thomas said, "No, I do not think that is true. I think the world is becoming a little churchy, but I think the church is becoming immensely worldly."

Since World War II there has been a breakdown of the wall of separation between the church and the world. The separation that many had practiced was legalistic and, I think, unscriptural. The church was like the little Dutch boy who was keeping his thumb in the dike.

Then, in the aftermath of the war, along came television, lawlessness, immorality, and juvenile delinquency; first the beatniks, then the hippies, then dope and marijuana, and the philosophy of existentialism. A tidal wave swept over the dikes of separation, and even the little Dutch boy was washed away.

There is no simple answer to the question: What is worldliness? But I am going to let James give what I think is his very definitive answer. What is worldliness? James says that worldliness is strife and envy. We need to go back to chapter 3 to pick up his thoughts. In James 3:13 we read, "Who is a wise man and endued with knowledge among you? Let him shew out of a good conversation his works with meekness of wisdom." Faith is the major in James' university, and all elective courses are related to faith. Works of faith bring meekness.Then we read, "But the wisdom that is from above is first pure, then peaceable, gentle" (James 3:17). There is meekness or humility, and humility means submission.

In James 3:16 we read, "For where envying and strife is, there is confusion and every evil work." That is worldliness. And worldliness in the church has produced all the cults, denominations, factions, divisions, and cliques which have arisen and abound in the church today. There is a spirit of rivalry and jealousy in the church. In the previous verse, James describes this as "earthly"—that is, it is confined to the earth. It is "sensual"—that is, psychological. And then it's "devilish" or demonic, which is something quite terrible, my friend.

What do envy and strife produce in this world? They produce "confusion and every evil work." With this as background, we can recognize what James is saying now in chapter 4—

From whence come wars and fightings among you? come they not hence, even of your lusts that war in your members? [James 4:1].

"Wars" have to do with the wars of nations. "Fightings" have to do with little skirmishes—that little fight you had in the church—you remember?

"Come they not hence even of your lusts that war in your members?" You wanted to have your own way. "Lusts that war in your members" are actually sensual pleasures. Strife and turmoil are created by conflicts and the overweening demands of the members of the body for satisfaction.

> **Ye lust, and have not: ye kill, and desire to have, and cannot obtain: ye fight and war, yet ye have not, because ye ask not [James 4:2].**

Selfish desires, James makes it very clear, lead to war. This spirit of strife is worldliness; it is not Christian, and it is not the Christian approach. These are the things which represent the old nature. A man must be regenerated by faith in Christ and be indwelt by the Holy Spirit.

What James describes here is the spirit of the world. When the spirit of the world gets into the church, you have a worldly church. My friend, do you think it is bad out on the battlefield? Did you think it was bad in Vietnam? Well, it was, but inside some churches and inside the hearts of some individuals it is just as bad. In the business world there is dog-eat-dog competition—that is worldliness. Political parties split, and one group becomes pitted against another. As capital and labor meet around the conference table, there is a battle going on. In the social world there are climbers on the social ladder who are stepping on the hands of others as they go up. In your neighborhood and mine one family does not speak to another family. Within families there are quarrels, brother against brother. Then that spirit gets into the church. *That*, my friend, is worldliness.

"Yet ye have not because ye ask not." Our desires should be taken to the Lord in prayer—to have them satisfied or denied or refined—and then we need to accept the answer from Him. What is the cure for worldliness? It is prayer. It is, therefore, faith in God. The apostle John put it like this, "For whatsoever is born of God overcometh the world: and this is the victory that overcometh the world, even our faith" (1 John 5:4). The answer is to trust in God absolutely, to go to Him in prayer and commit to Him that which is in your heart. When you find that there is strife and envy in your heart, talk to Him about it. Many of us go to the Lord to tell Him how good we are. And because we have been good little boys and girls who have gone to Sunday School, we think He ought to give us a lollipop or a Brownie button or something of that sort. My friend, we need to get right down to the nitty-gritty where we live. Consider these words which were written by a great saint, a mystic of the Middle Ages, Fénelon:

> Tell God all that is in your heart, as one unloads one's heart, its pleasures and its pains, to a dear friend. Tell Him your troubles, that He may comfort you; tell Him your joys, that He may sober them; tell Him your longings, that He may purify them; tell Him your dislikes, that He may help you to conquer them; talk to Him of your temptations, that He may shield you from them; show Him the wounds of your heart, that He may heal them; lay bare your indifference to good, your depraved tastes for evil, your instability. Tell Him how self-love makes you unjust to others, how vanity tempts you to be insincere, how pride disguises you to yourself as to others.
>
> If you thus pour out all your weaknesses, needs, troubles, there will be no lack of what to say. You will never exhaust the subject. It is continually being renewed. People who have no secrets from each other never want subjects of conversation. They do not weigh their words, for there is nothing to be held back; neither do they seek for something to say. They talk out of the abundance of the heart, without consideration, just what they think. Blessed are they who attain to such familiar, unreserved intercourse with God.

When I was laid aside for some time with an illness, I found that all things do work together for good. My wife and I were able to sit at home for a longer period of time than we ever had since we were married. Even on our honeymoon I candidated at a church. From that day to this we have been on the go. We found that there were some things we really needed to talk over that otherwise might have been misunderstood. We had wonderful talks, and we just laid bare our hearts to each other. It was the most joyous experience. I said to her, "Honey, this is more wonderful than our honeymoon was!" That is the kind of relationship we ought to have with God.

Having studied the Word of God and having read these words by Fénelon, I came to the conclusion that I was going to tell the Lord Jesus everything. I have talked to Him about everything in my life that was sinful and questionable. He knows, He understands, and He's forgiven me.

The only way to take away that envy and jealousy and strife which is in your heart is to go to the Lord Jesus. You don't need to go to the psychiatrist; he'll just move your problem from one area to another. You need to get rid of that hang-up by going to the Lord Jesus, getting on *His* couch, and telling Him everything.

James says that the solution is for you and me to pray, but we often pray for selfish ends—

> **Ye ask, and receive not, because ye ask amiss, that ye may consume it upon your lusts [James 4:3].**

Even when we do ask God for something, we ask in order that we might spend it in a very selfish way.

> **Ye adulterers and adulteresses, know ye not that the friendship of the world is enmity with God? whosoever therefore will be a friend of the world is the enemy of God [James 4:4].**

Because we are willing to compromise with the world in order to attain our goals, James calls us "adulterers and adulteresses." This is the way of the world: take by force what you want; by hook or by crook lay hold of it; be envious and jealous of other folk, and cause strife. That is worldliness.

"Know ye not that the friendship of the world is enmity with God?" I have never joined any of the clubs or lodges such as the Lions, the Moose, the Elks, or the Rotary Club. I have been asked to join, but I do not join them. I'll tell you the reason. I have enough trouble with worldliness in the church; I do not need to join a worldly organization.

Do ye think that the scripture saith in vain, The spirit that dwelleth in us lusteth to envy? [James 4:5].

Are we trying to kid ourselves that we are nice, sweet, little folk who have no envy and jealousy in our hearts? I heard a woman say one time, "I have a very wonderful husband. He is not jealous of me." I want you to know that something is wrong if a husband is not jealous of his wife. If he loves her, he will be jealous of her. God says that He is jealous of His children. But what about jealousy in the wrong sense—jealousy when we do not get elected to a committee or do not receive recognition in the church that we feel we deserve? And what about the strife we cause with these tongues of ours? James says that the solution to the problem is to go to the Lord Jesus and tell Him about our problem, tell Him everything.

But he giveth more grace. Wherefore he saith, God resisteth the proud, but giveth grace unto the humble [James 4:6].

I have said this again and again: God is overloaded with grace. You and I just don't know how gracious He is. He has an abundance of grace. *Grace* has been defined as unmerited favor, but I call it love in action. God didn't save us by love. He gave His Son, and it is by His grace that we are saved. He has so much of it. You may say, "Oh, I am so wrong on the inside, so sinful." Go to Him and tell Him you are wrong on the inside, and ask Him for grace to overcome it. He will give you grace. He is the living Christ, interceding at God's right hand for you.

Now some may doubt the surplus of His grace. May I say to you, all the medicine in the world cannot cure the sick; the remedy *must be taken*. Likewise, God has the grace, my friend; lay hold of it! It is possible for a man to die of thirst with a pure spring of water right before him. He has to drink of it; he has to appropriate it before it can save his life. You don't blame soap and water for the fact that there are dirty people in the world, do you? There is plenty of soap and water to clean you up, my friend.

"God resisteth the proud, but giveth grace unto the humble." This is the kind of container that the grace of God must be carried in; it must be carried in an humble individual.

> **Submit yourselves therefore to God. Resist the devil, and he will flee from you [James 4:7].**

When you go to a doctor for medical care, you submit yourself to him. One time when I was sick, the doctor gave me half a dozen prescriptions. The man might have been trying to poison me, but I had faith in him and took his pills. They helped me because I submitted to him. "Submit yourselves therefore to God."

"Resist the devil, and he will flee from you." You may ask, "How am I going to resist the Devil?" James is going to be very practical. He has just said that we need a little more grace—He "giveth grace unto the humble." In other words, you are not going to be able to resist the Devil in your own strength. You and I are surrounded by evil influences. Temptation, as we have seen, is on every hand. God supplies His grace as needed, and His supply never runs out. "This is yours," God says. "You are to lay hold of it."

> **Draw nigh to God, and he will draw nigh to you. Cleanse your hands, ye sinners; and purify your hearts, ye double minded [James 4:8].**

God comes to the door of your heart; He will not come any farther. He knocks, and you have to let Him in. That is the only way He is going to get in, my friend.

It is said that one time Martin Luther threw an inkwell at the Devil. Somebody might say that was a crazy thing to do, but it is not if you are resisting the Devil. James tells us that the way to resist the Devil is to draw near to God. The Devil will flee from you, because he doesn't like God as company. The Devil will not get to you unless you get too far away from God. A wolf never attacks a sheep as long as it is with the rest of the sheep and with the shepherd. And the closer the sheep is to the shepherd, the safer it is. Our problem is that we get too far from God.

> **Be afflicted, and mourn, and weep: let your laughter be turned to mourning, and your joy to heaviness [James 4:9].**

There are certain conditions which call for mourning and not for joy. Sin is never to be treated lightly. When I hear a Christian make light of sin, I have a sneaking notion that, on the side, when nobody is looking, he is indulging in sin. You are not to treat sin lightly, my friend; you are to *mourn* over your sins. The problem today is that Christians are not mourning over their sins.

We have several outstanding evangelists and some great evangelistic meetings in our day, but why is it that there is no revival in the church? I think James is giving us something to think about in what he says here. I remember asking this same question of Dr. John Brown, who was one of the great evangelists in the past. As we sat on his front porch in Siloam Springs, Arkansas, I asked him why, even in that day, evangelism was not reviving the church as it had when he was active in the ministry. He told me about the meetings which he had held in my present hometown of Pasadena, California, where he had a tent set up on a big vacant lot at the corner of Washington and Holliston. He said this to me, "Dr. McGee, I preached six weeks to the Christians before I ever attempted to give an altar call for the unsaved—and revival came to the churches." When I came as pastor to a church in Pasadena, I could still see the effects of Dr. Brown's meetings in that church. Why? For the very simple reason that sin had been dealt with in the lives of believers. Too often we refuse to deal with it. We need to mourn over our sins.

> **Humble yourselves in the sight of the Lord, and he shall lift you up [James 4:10].**

"*He* shall lift you up." This is our problem today: We think *we* are smart. We think *we* are strong. We think *we* have ability. We think *we* are good. God says that there is no good within us. There is nothing in us that attracts Him, that is, in the way of goodness; it is just our great need that draws Him to us. If we are willing to humble ourselves and get down where He can lift us up, He will lift us up.

I observed a lifeguard once as he hit a drowning fellow with his fist and knocked him out. The lifeguard explained that the drowning man was struggling and that he could not help him until he gave up. I think sometimes God gives us the fist so that we just give up and let Him take over.

> **Speak not evil one of another, brethren. He that speaketh evil of his brother, and judgeth his brother, speaketh evil of the law, and judgeth the law: but if thou judge the law, thou art not a doer of the law, but a judge.**
>
> **There is one lawgiver, who is able to save and to destroy: who art thou that judgest another? [James 4:11–12].**

If you judge your brother, you disobey the law, which is putting yourself above the law and treating it with contempt. In other words, who do you think you are? When you begin to talk like that, you are moving into the position of God. There are two types of people today who seek to take the position of God. One is the sinner who says, "I'm good enough to be saved. Lord, I don't need your salvation. You just move over, and I am going to move up and sit beside you. I am my own savior." But, my friend, God says in His Word that He is the only Savior. Then there is the other fellow who sits in judgment on everyone else. He doesn't judge himself, but he judges everyone else. James is saying that judgment is God's business. Jesus said, "For the Father judgeth no man, but hath committed all judgment unto the Son" (John 5:22). There are many Christians who, in effect, say to the Lord Jesus, "You move over, I'm going to help You. We are going to have a Supreme Court, and I am going to be one of the judges." We have a lot of believers like that today; boy, what a Supreme Court the church could furnish Him! James says that we are to judge ourselves and to go to Him in humility.

> **Go to now, ye that say, Today or tomorrow we will go into such a city, and continue there a year, and buy and sell, and get gain [James 4:13].**

Here is something else Christians do—we like to make big plans for the future. It has taken me a long time in life to learn just to play it by ear. Normally I accept speaking engagements quite some time ahead of schedule, but in periods of serious illness I have been forced to cancel some engagements. I have hated to cancel them, but the Lord has brought this passage of Scripture to my mind: "Come now, ye that say, Today or tomorrow we will go into such a city and hold a Bible conference. We will have a wonderful time there, and we believe it is the Lord's will." That is not exactly what James said, but that is how the Lord has said it to me.

> **Whereas ye know not what shall be on the morrow. For what is your life? It is even a vapour, that appeareth for a little time, and then vanisheth away [James 4:14].**

James says that we do not know what tomorrow holds. "For what is your life?" He says it is just a vapor, a fog. "It is even a vapour, that appeareth for a little time, and then vanisheth away." We have a lot of fog here on the West Coast. You can be driving along the coast on a marvelous day when the ocean is as blue as indigo and the sky almost as blue as the ocean, but if you stop at a motel for the night, you may find in the morning that everything is shrouded by fog. Life is like a mist on a mountainside—uncertain, transient, and temporary.

Human life lived apart from and without God is the most colossal failure in God's universe. Everything else serves a long and useful purpose. The sun in the sky is prodigal of its energy—we use very little of it. The moon also serves a purpose; many of you fellows got married because of that moon up there. It is the poet who said, "Only man is vile." Human life apart from God is out of joint, dislocated, a colossal failure. One of the reasons is the brevity of this life. We are allotted only three score and ten years; if we get any more, they are filled with aches and pains. Oh, the brevity of human life! Many of us never learn to really live down here upon this earth.

> **For that ye ought to say, If the Lord will, we shall live, and do this, or that [James 4:15].**

Our lives are in the hand of God.

> **But now ye rejoice in your boastings: all such rejoicing is evil [James 4:16].**

Man cannot boast; if he does, it is sin.

> **Therefore to him that knoweth to do good, and doeth it not, to him it is sin [James 4:17].**

There are a great many people today who are sinning and don't know it. If you know to do good in certain cases—if you know that you should do a certain thing or help a certain cause—and you do not do it, *that* is sin.

Our lives are brief, and we should not spend our time in strife and envy and jealousy. It spoils a life. We need to come to Christ, put our lives down before Him, and really start living. He has said, ". . . I am come that they might have life, and that they might have it more abundantly" (John 10:10). He wants to give you a life that is a life indeed. Are you living that life today?

CHAPTER 5

THEME: Riches are a care; the coming of Christ is a comfort; the prayer of the righteous is a power

RICHES ARE A CARE

We have come to a remarkable section of the Epistle of James which may seem out of place in this epistle. A cursory reading of these first six verses might give the impression that James is teaching a socialistic doctrine of "soak the rich" or "let's divide the wealth." But on the contrary, a careful reading of these verses reveals that James is not teaching any such thing. He was instructing believers as to their attitude and action in a world that was going to the bowwows, a world filled with injustice, where freedom was only a dream. The Roman world of James' day was not like the modern world in which we live. The life-styles were entirely different. There was no middle class in the days of James. There were the very rich, the filthy rich, and the very poor, the filthy poor. The majority of the Christians of that day came from the very poor and slave classes. They had no great cathedrals on boulevards, and they were not building kingdoms as are many of these great churches which are spending millions of dollars these days. The early church just wasn't that kind of church.

As we approach this passage of Scripture, we should understand that James is not condemning riches. Riches in themselves are not immoral; they are not moral, either. They are just unmoral or amoral. The Bible actually does not condemn money. A great many people have the viewpoint that there is something dirty about money; they call it "filthy lucre." Scripture doesn't say that. What Scripture does say is that " . . . the love of money is the root of all evil . . ." (1 Tim. 6:10). The problem is not in the coin; the problem is in the hearts of men and women. It is the *love* of money that is the root of all evil. James was not condemning people just because they were rich but because of their wrong relationship to their riches. He was concerned with how they got their money and what they were doing with it after they got it.

The Lord Jesus Christ had a great deal to say about money and about riches. He gave three parables which I think will help us to understand what James is saying. In Luke 16:19–31 we have the story (which I think is a true story) of the poor man, Lazarus the beggar, and the rich man. This parable has to do with the way the richman spent his money. He was really living it up. It is interesting that this beggar, Lazarus, was placed at his gate. Who put him there? I don't know, but in some way the rich man was responsible for him. And the rich man let the beggar have the crumbs from his table. May I say to you, I would wager that the rich man deducted those crumbs from his income tax! Nevertheless, we are told that the dogs licked the beggar's sores while the rich man "fared sumptuously." It was the way this man became rich that in some way made him responsible for the beggar's condition. Someone will ask, "What makes you think that?" Well, where did the two men go after death? Lazarus went to Abraham's Bosom, and the rich man went to hell. That shows us how God judged the lives of these two men, my friend.

In Luke 12 the Lord Jesus gave a second parable about a rich man. This man is the one who built bigger barns—at least he had plans to build them. However, he never did build the barns because he died. The Lord Jesus Christ never condemned that man for being rich; when He stated it, He just stated it as a fact. To all outward appearances, this man was a good man and an honest citizen. But he hoarded his money. He wanted to live it up in his old age, and he gave no thought to eternity. The Lord Jesus called him a fool. Actually, he was more than covetous; he was selfish. He was hoarding his money for himself, and that, may I say, is a form of idolatry. We are told in the Word of God that covetousness is idolatry; it is the worship of things. But selfishness is when you worship yourself.

There is a lot of that going on today; in fact, it is even being taught as a Christian virtue. We are told that we are to have great respect for ourselves and great confidence in ourselves. But the Lord Jesus said, " . . . without me ye can do nothing" (John 15:5).

There is a third parable concerning riches which the Lord Jesus gave. It is the parable of the unjust steward by which we are taught the wise use of money by Christians. God holds man responsible not only for how he makes his money but also for how he spends it.

There is another question we should consider before we examine the text: Are the rich whom James is condemning here Christians or non-Christians? Are they the godly rich or the godless rich? There is some controversy and difference of opinion among commentators on this question. I personally believe that they are the godless rich, and in that I follow the opinion of one whom I respect a great deal, John Calvin. Thomas Manton writes that it was Calvin's judgment that "these six verses are not so much an admonition as a denunciation, wherein the apostle doth not so much direct them what to do, as fore-tell what should be done to them, that the godly might be encouraged to the more patience under their oppressions; for that the apostle infer-reth plainly."

Why does James turn from talking to the godly and begin talking to the ungodly? The fact of the matter is that he doesn't change. He is still speaking to the godly. How can that be, when he is so obviously speaking to the rich? As he speaks to the ungodly, he is at the same time telling the godly that they live in a godless world, where the god-less rich will impose certain hardships upon them and take advantage of them and where they will be at the mercy of these wicked, rich men. The Lord Jesus Christ had already made a general reference to this when He said, " . . . In the world ye shall have tribulation [trouble]: but be of good cheer; I have overcome the world" (John 16:33).

The godly are to be patient in these circumstances, knowing that God will deal with the godless rich in eternity if not here. This is made very clear in verse 6 of this chapter: "Ye have condemned and killed the just"—God condemns these actions of the rich; "and he doth not resist you"—but God permits them, so it seems, to get by with it. How-ever, He will judge them in the end. May I make this rather startling statement. I would rather go to hell a poor man than a rich man. But I thank God that I am not going there, and that is because Christ died for me and I have accepted His gift of eternal life.

David was troubled by the prosperity of the wicked; it bothered him no end. In Psalm 37:35-36 we read, "I have seen the wicked in great power, and spreading himself like a green bay tree. Yet he passed away, and, lo, he was not: yea, I sought him, but he could not be found." Earlier in this psalm, David gives the same advice that James gives: "Rest in the LORD, and wait patiently for him: fret not thyself because of him who prospereth in his way, because of the man who bringeth wicked devices to pass" (Ps. 37:7). That is a tremendous statement, and he is speaking of the godless rich. David was troubled by this until he went into the temple and saw that, in time, God would deal with these people.

Let us come now to the text—

Go to now, ye rich men, weep and howl for your miseries that shall come upon you [James 5:1].

Is James speaking to the godless rich of his day or of some future day? He is giving a warning to the rich in his day, and it has an application for *any* day and certainly for our day. James wrote this epistle, we believe, somewhere between A.D. 45 and 50. Many others now give the date as A.D. 60. Regardless of the date, the destruction of Jerusalem was in the near future, for in A.D. 70 Titus the Roman came and destroyed Jerusalem as it had never been destroyed before. He plowed it under. He hated Christians and he hated Jews, and they both were in that city. Believe me, when he got through, there were no rich Jews left. They had either been killed or had been put in slavery, and all the riches had been destroyed or lost or confiscated. James can make these strong statements in view of what was coming, for the Lord Jesus had predicted this before He ascended back to heaven. He told His disciples, "And when ye shall see Jerusalem compassed with armies, then know that the desolation thereof is nigh" (Luke 21:20). That was fulfilled in A.D. 70.

Your riches are corrupted, and your garments are motheaten [James 5:2].

In light of the coming of Christ, they are warned that all the riches of the world will come to naught. This obviously would not impress a godless rich person in that day any more than it would today; however, the rich man knew that the future was uncertain for him, just as many realize that today. There is always a danger of a panic, a crash, a drought, or a depression. That has been the order of the day since men started to mint money.

There will always be good years, and there will always be bad years. Some of us can remember the depression of the early 1930s when millionaires by the score leaped out of the windows of sky-scrapers, and many rich found that they became paupers overnight. Some former millionaires sold apples at street corners, and gilt-edged stocks and bonds in safety deposit boxes were not worth the paper they were written on.

> **Your gold and silver is cankered; and the rust of them shall be a witness against you, and shall eat your flesh as it were fire. Ye have heaped treasure together for the last days [James 5:3].**

James says, "Do you know how your silver and gold are going to rust? It is because *you* are going to decay." This is the judgment that comes upon the godless rich like the men in two of the parables which Christ gave. Death came to both of them, and death certainly separates a rich man from his money. It is said that when one of the Vanderbilts was dying, the family was waiting in an outer room. When the lawyer and the doctor came out, one of the more outspoken members of the family stepped up to the lawyer and asked, "How much did he leave?" The lawyer replied, "He left it all. He didn't take any of it with him." May I say to you, that is the way that it rusts, my friend. A gentleman was being shown through the magnificent grounds of a rich nobleman's estate, and he said to the owner, "Well, my lord, all this and heaven would be noble; but this and hell would be terrible."

James is condemning the godless rich for hoarding their money. Gold and silver *do* rust. It's boom today and bust tomorrow. When a man makes a million, he is not satisfied with that. He wants to make *two* million. It's like drinking sea water—the more you drink, the thirstier you get. The rich keep on making millions, but it doesn't make them any happier.

We had here in America two men who were billionaires whose lives are an example of the futility of riches. Both of them were remarkable men who built great financial empires. Howard Hughes was one of them, but in his last days, from all we can learn, he was a recluse and a sick man. He could not have been happy in those years. All that money just didn't seem to do him very much good. The other man, J. Paul Getty, was reported in the press to have made this statement: "I'd give all my wealth for just one happy marriage." How tragic!

God gave wealth not to be hoarded but to be dispensed. The rich man in Christ's parable planned to build bigger barns in which to store his goods and his fruits. But you can eat only so much; you can drink only so much, and you can wear only one suit at a time. After the first million dollars, when you start gathering more millions, they are just like a pile of rocks. You cannot eat them; there is nothing you can do with them. That is the reason our Lord called that man a fool. Instead of filling his own barn, he should have gone and filled someone else's barn.

I know a Christian farmer who lives in the fruit belt of California. He told me that the organization of farmers to which he belonged asked him to dump some of his fruit crop in order to keep the prices up. He said that tons of fruit had been destroyed. There were a lot of folk who could have used and enjoyed that fruit. James says that wealth is to be dispensed and not hoarded.

Let me pass on to you two little stories which have come my way. A certain young person very impatiently said, "I'm living now, and I mean to have a good time. The hereafter isn't here yet!" A very wise companion replied, "No—only the first part of it; but I shouldn't wonder if the 'here' had a good deal to do with shaping the 'after.'"

There was an irreligious farmer who gloried in the fact that he was an agnostic. He wrote a letter to a local newspaper, saying, "Sir, I have been trying an experiment with a field of mine. I plowed it on Sunday. I planted it on Sunday. I cultivated it on Sunday. I reaped it on Sunday. I hauled it into my barn on Sunday. And now, Mr. Editor, what is the result? I have more bushels to the acre in that field than any of my neighbors have had this October." The editor wasn't a religious man himself, but he published the letter and then wrote below it: "God does not always settle His accounts in October." God has eternity ahead of Him, my friend.

> **Behold, the hire of the labourers who have reaped down your fields, which is of you kept back by fraud, crieth: and the cries of them which have reaped are entered into the ears of the Lord of sabaoth [James 5:4].**

James condemns the godless rich not only for hoarding money but for making it in a dishonest way. They have robbed the poor to get rich. In the parable, the rich man let fall some crumbs for the beggar. What a message is in that! That beggar had been placed at the rich man's gate because the rich man was responsible for him.

In Proverbs 22:7 it says, "The rich ruleth over the poor, and the borrower is servant to the lender." God condemns the godless man who makes his money in a dishonest way, especially when it is by putting down the children of God. God may do nothing now, but He is going to judge in the future. If men are making their riches by stepping on the hands of those beneath them, then God will judge that. This should serve as a word of warning to the rich man, to great corporations and labor unions, and also to great church organizations. God will judge the way men make their money and the way they spend it.

> **Ye have lived in pleasure on the earth, and been wanton; ye have nourished your hearts, as in a day of slaughter [James 5:5].**

The rich were spending their money in a sinful manner. The miser says, "Dollars are flat to stack them," but the spendthrift says, "They are round to roll them." Either way, God says that you are wrong, my friend.

Again, let me quote a proverb: "The rich man's wealth is his strong city, and as an high wall in his own conceit" (Prov. 18:11). Then in Proverbs 28:11 we read, "The rich man is wise in his own conceit; but the poor that hath understanding searcheth him out." This is the picture of the two godless rich men whom the Lord Jesus told about; both wanted to live it up. One wanted to store it up now and then live it up in his old age. The other rich man was living it up at the time while the beggar lay outside his gate. If you have decided to live for this life only, be sure to live it up, but God says you are a fool, my friend.

Ye have condemned and killed the just; and he doth not resist you [James 5:6].

"Ye have condemned and killed the just." When we look about us at our own government and the other governments of the world, it would seem that there is a power structure which manipulates government and which manipulates the economy. We hear a great deal about the freedom of the press, but that freedom is a freedom to brainwash people to their way of thinking. Although we are supposed to have freedom of speech and of religion, on the most powerful radio stations in any city in this country, you cannot buy time on weekdays for the teaching of the Word of God. That is true no matter how much money you might have to pay for it.

"And he doth not resist you." The rich seem to be getting by with it today, and the sinner is getting by with it. That disturbed David at first. He said, "They spread themselves like a green bay tree and do not cease from flourishing." If I do something wrong, I get punished for it. God takes me to the woodshed, but the king of Babylon just keeps on going and nothing stops him. Actually, that is God's judgment on the wicked. He is not judging them now, but the end to which they come is very terrible. Riches have never brought happiness to mankind at all.

There is a lesson here for the rich man who is a Christian. How big is your bank account? If Jesus should come right now, would you be willing to let Him look into your safety deposit box? He is going to do that someday. How are you making use of your riches?

Proverbs 30:8 says, ". . . give me neither poverty nor riches; feed me with food convenient for me." I am thankful that I am neither rich nor poor, because if I were rich, I would forget God, and if I were poor, I might steal. I thank God that I can go down the middle of the road today in the middle class.

THE COMING OF CHRIST IS A COMFORT

James had made it very clear what kind of world we live in. It's a big, bad world with a dog-eat-dog philosophy. Those who are climbing up the ladder of riches are stepping on the fingers of others as they go up. Should Christians join some organization and go all out for good government? Certainly we ought to be interested in trying to elect the best men. However, we cannot change this world, my friend. What, then, can we do? Listen to God; He is speaking now to His own children—

> **Be patient therefore, brethren, unto the coming of the Lord. Behold, the husbandman waiteth for the precious fruit of the earth, and hath long patience for it, until he receive the early and latter rain [James 5:7].**

The Word of God has a great deal to say about the fact that when Christ comes and sets up His kingdom, the poor are going to get a good deal, a right and honest deal, for the first time in the history of the world. This is something that all of the prophets mentioned and which they emphasized. In Isaiah 11:4 we read, "But with righteousness shall he judge the poor. . . ." Believe me, the poor have not had a good deal yet. If you think that by changing a political party you will somehow get a good deal for the poor, you are wrong. I don't mean to be a pessimist, my friend, but you simply cannot look to mankind, to men who are grasping for power and money, and expect them to act righteously. It does not matter what they promise, they are not going to take care of the poor. Our only hope is in Jesus Christ. If there is any group of people who ought to be interested in the Lord Jesus Christ, it is the poor people of this world, because He is going to give them the right kind of deal when He establishes His kingdom here upon earth.

"Be patient therefore, brethren, unto the coming of the Lord." This is a tremendous statement. The coming of Christ will correct the wrongs of the world. We can read this again and again in Scripture. Not only do the prophets mention it, but Christ Himself made it clear in the Sermon on the Mount (which will be the law of His kingdom) that He intends to give the poor a square deal under His reign (see Matt. 6:19–24).

"Behold, the husbandman waiteth for the precious fruit of the earth, and hath long patience for it, until he receive the early and latter rain." In other words, when the farmer plants his grain, he doesn't go out the next morning to see if it is time to harvest it. James says, "Be patient. The harvest is coming."

We often hear it said that Christians are *harvesting* when they go out in evangelism to give out the Word of God. I disagree with that. The Lord Jesus was at the end of an age when He said to His disciples (He was sending them out to the lost sheep of the house of Israel, not worldwide), ". . . The harvest truly is great, but the labourers are few . . ." (Luke 10:2). They were at the end of the age of law. Every age has ended in judgment; the present age will end in a judgment from God. *That* will be the harvest. In Matthew 13 the Lord Jesus said that He will send His angels to do the gathering in for the harvest. Believers do not harvest. *He* is the one who separates the wheat from the tares. Therefore, what are we doing when we give out the Word of God? The Lord Jesus is also a sower, and today He is sowing seed. I consider that to be my business. I teach the Word of God, and there is nothing in the world I can do but simply give it out. I'm just sowing seed. Some falls on good ground. Maybe not too much of it, but some falls on good ground. Hallelujah for that! Our business is growing seed.

> **Be ye also patient; stablish your hearts: for the coming of the Lord draweth nigh [James 5:8].**

All the way through Scripture we are taught that we should live in the light of the coming of Christ.

> **Grudge not one against another, brethren, lest ye be condemned: behold, the judge standeth before the door [James 5:9].**

It would be very embarrassing if the Lord should come while you are sitting in judgment on someone else. You would suddenly find yourself in His presence with Him judging you. What James is really saying here is, "Set your house in order. Get your affairs straightened out before He comes, because He is going to straighten them out if you don't." This is very important for believers to realize.

> **Take, my brethren, the prophets, who have spoken in the name of the Lord, for an example of suffering affliction, and of patience [James 5:10].**

The prophets are an example to us. They suffered, and they were patient.

> **Behold, we count them happy which endure. Ye have heard of the patience of Job, and have seen the end of the Lord; that the Lord is very pitiful, and of tender mercy [James 5:11].**

"Ye have heard of the patience of Job." That is about all I know about Job's patience—I've *heard* of it. As I read the Book of Job, I feel Job was very impatient. Actually, he *learned* patience. He was an impatient man, but he learned patience.

"And have seen the end of the Lord; that the Lord is very pitiful, and of tender mercy." In other words, the Lord is full of pity or compassion and is merciful. You have to go to the end of Job's trial to see that he learned a great lesson and that the Lord was indeed compassionate and generous with him.

> **But above all things, my brethren, swear not, neither by heaven, neither by the earth, neither by any other oath: but let your yea be yea; and your nay, nay; lest ye fall into condemnation [James 5:12].**

In other words, my friend, when you say you are going to promise something, it ought to be as if you were in a courtroom and had taken an oath to tell the truth. All your *conversation* ought to be like that. I can remember when my dad went to the bank one year to borrow money to get his cotton gin started. The banker was busy and said to my dad, "Go ahead and take the money." My dad said, "But I haven't signed the note." I never shall forget what the banker said, "If you *say* you will repay it, that is just as good as if you have signed a note. So come in later and sign up." May I say to you, a man's word ought to be just that good. Some people, even if they take an oath on a stack of Bibles, do not honor their word.

THE PRAYER OF THE RIGHTEOUS IS A POWER

Is any among you afflicted? let him pray. Is any merry? let him sing psalms [James 5:13].

James says that the afflicted are to pray and the merry are to sing psalms. Sometimes a song leader will get up in a service and say, "Now everybody sit up and smile." I used to have a song leader like that in a church I pastored years ago. I told him, "Don't you know that in this congregation there are people who are really burdened? As I look out there, I see one man who is a doctor and who has been busy all week taking care of patients. I also see a lady who is a buyer in a department store. She is weary and tired. And you ask them to sit up and smile!" No, you don't have to sit up and smile. The afflicted are to pray. The merry are to sing psalms. Some people go to church and then try to work up some enthusiasm. We ought to have the great passion and enthusiasm in our hearts even before we go to church, but we do not need to put on a false front.

Is any sick among you? let him call for the elders of the church; and let them pray over him, anointing him with oil in the name of the Lord [James 5:14].

A few years ago there was a tragic incident which occurred in a little town near Los Angeles where a man threw away the insulin that his little son was supposed to take because he said God was going to heal his son. The little fellow died, and then the man, who must be very fanatic, said, "The Lord is going to raise him up from the dead because he has been anointed." The leaders of the denomination to which the man belonged said that he had never been taught anything like that. I believe that is true because I have had the privilege of meeting on several occasions with the man who taught theology in one of the outstanding Pentecostal schools. He said this to me, "Dr. McGee, I want you to know that I agree with you that not everyone can be healed. It must be the will of God in order for someone to be healed." That is my position, and I agree with what he said.

If you say that it is God's will for every Christian who gets sick to be healed, you must agree that the logical conclusion of that line of thinking is that the Christian will never die. He will be healed of every disease which causes death. May I say, that is ridiculous. I have been healed of cancer, but I expect to die, if the Lord does not come in the meantime. It is a cruel hoax perpetrated upon simple believers that it is God's will for *all* to be healed.

James is not actually asking a question here. He is saying, "Someone is sick among you." What are you to do? "Let him call for the elders of the church; and let them pray over him"—that's the first thing. The second thing is—"anointing him with oil in the name of the Lord."

There are two Greek words which are translated "anoint" in the New Testament. One of them is used in a religious sense; that word is *chriō* in the Greek. From that we get the word *Christos*; Christ was the Anointed One. It means to anoint with some scented unguent or oil. It is used only five times in the New Testament, and it refers to the anointing of Christ by God the Father with the Holy Spirit.

The second word translated "anoint" is *aleiphō*. It is used a number of times in the New Testament. In Matthew 6:17 we read, "But thou, when thou fastest, anoint thine head, and wash thy face." That simply means to put oil on your hair so that you will look all right. Trench comments that *aleiphō* is "the mundane and profane word." The other, *chriō*, is "the sacred and religious word." The word used in this verse in James is *aleiphō*, and all it means is to rub with oil. You remember that when Hezekiah was sick, they put something medicinal on that boil he had. James is saying something very practical here. He says, "Call for the elders to pray, and go to the best doctor you can get." You *are* to use medicine, my friend. It is a mistaken idea to say that this refers to some religious ceremony of putting a little oil from a bottle on someone's head, as if that would have some healing merit in it. It has no merit whatsoever. James is too practical for that.

James is also a man of prayer. He says, "Call for the elders to pray." This is the reason that when I get sick I ask others to pray. I believe in the priesthood of believers. James makes this very clear in the following verses—

> **And the prayer of faith shall save the sick, and the Lord shall raise him up; and if he have committed sins, they shall be forgiven him.**

> **Confess your faults one to another, and pray one for another, that ye may be healed. The effectual fervent prayer of a righteous man availeth much [James 5:15-16].**

"And the prayer of faith shall save the sick." I believe you are to call on God's people to pray for you when you are sick.

"Confess your faults one to another and pray one for another, that ye may be healed." We are to confess our sins to God but our faults one to another. If I have injured you, then I ought to confess that to you. But I will not confess my sins to you, and I do not want you confessing your sins to me. You are to confess that to the Lord. "If we confess our sins, he is faithful and just to forgive us our sins, and to cleanse us from all unrighteousness" (1 John 1:9). I cannot forgive sins: neither can any clergyman forgive sins—only God can do that.

"The effectual fervent prayer of a righteous man availeth much." James was a great man of prayer. He was called "Old Camel Knees" because, having spent so much time on his knees in prayer, his knees were calloused. He speaks now of another great man of prayer, Elijah (*Elias* is the Greek form of *Elijah*)—

> **Elias was a man subject to like passions as we are, and he prayed earnestly that it might not rain: and it rained not on the earth by the space of three years and six months.**

> **And he prayed again, and the heaven gave rain, and the earth brought forth her fruit [James 5:17–18].**

Can you imagine that? Elijah was a weatherman for three and a half years, and for three and a half years he held back the rain! It did not come until he prayed. You are the same kind of person Elijah was. Elijah wasn't a superman; he was "a man subject to like passions as we are." But he was a man who prayed with passion, and that is the kind of praying we need today.

> **Brethren, if any of you do err from the truth, and one convert him;**

> **Let him know, that he which converteth the sinner from the error of his way shall save a soul from death, and shall hide a multitude of sins [James 5:19–20].**

"Converteth the sinner from the error of his way." Some expositors believe that this refers to a child of God who has gone astray. However, I believe it refers to an unsaved person who has not yet come to the truth.

"Shall hide a multitude of sins." When he comes to a saving knowledge of Christ, his sins—though they be multitudinous—will be covered by the blood of Christ. The wonder of justifcation by faith is that once God has pardoned our sins, they are gone forever—removed from us as far as the east is from the west.

This is a wonderful conclusion for this very practical Epistle of James.

BIBLIOGRAPHY

(Recommended for Further Study)

Adamson, James. *The Epistle of James*. Grand Rapids, Michigan: Wm. B. Eerdmans Publishing Co., 1976. (For advanced students)

Brown, Charles. *The Epistle of James*. London: The Religious Tract Society, 1907. (Devotional)

Criswell, W. A. *Expository Sermons on the Epistle of James*. Grand Rapids, Michigan: Zondervan Publishing House, 1975.

Gaebelein, Frank E. *The Practical Epistle of James*. Great Neck, New York: Doniger & Raughley, 1955.

Gwinn, Ralph A. *The Epistle of James*. Grand Rapids, Michigan: Baker Book House, 1967. (Shield Bible Study Series)

Hiebert, D. Edmond. *The Epistle of James*. Chicago, Illinois: Moody Press, 1979. (Highly recommended)

Ironside, H. A. *Notes on James and Peter*. Neptune, New Jersey: Loizeaux Brothers, n.d.

Johnstone, Robert. *Lectures on the Epistle of James*. Grand Rapids, Michigan: Baker Book House, 1871. (Comprehensive)

Kelly, William. *The Epistle of James*. London: G. Morrish, n.d.

King, Guy H. *A Belief That Behaves*. (Fort Washington, Pennsylvania: Christian Literature Crusade, 1945. (Excellent)

Knowling, R. J. *The Epistle of St. James*. London: Methusen, 1904.

Luck, G. Coleman. *James, Faith in Action*. Chicago, Illinois: Moody Press, 1954. (A fine, inexpensive survey)

Neibor, J. *Practical Exposition of James*. Erie, Pennsylvania: Our Daily Walk Publishers, 1950.

Plummer, Alfred. *The General Epistles of St. James and St. Jude.* Grand Rapids, Michigan: Wm. B. Eerdmans Publishing Co., n.d. (Expositor's Bible)

Robertson, A. T. *Studies in the Epistles of James.* Nashville, Tennessee: Broadman Press, 1915. (Excellent)

Strauss, Lehman. *James, Your Brother.* Neptune, New Jersey: Loizeaux Brothers, 1956. (Very practical)

Tasker, R. V. G. *The General Epistle of James.* Grand Rapids, Michigan: Wm. B. Eerdmans Pulishing Co., 1957. (Tyndale Commentary series)

Vaughan, Curtis. *James, A Study Guide.* Grand Rapids, Michigan: Zondervan Publishing House, 1969.

Zodhiates, Spiro. *The Behavior of Belief.* Grand Rapids, Michigan: Wm. B. Eerdmans Publishing Co., 1970. (Comprehensive)